The New Women of Color Daily Devotional Spring/Summer

The articles and prayers are taken from the *Women of Color Devotional Bible* © World Bible / Nia Publishing Co.

Urban Spirit! Publishing and Media Company is an African American owned company based in Atlanta, GA. You can find more information at http://www.urbanspirit.biz/

The New Women of Color Daily Devotional Spr/Sum Edition © Urban Spirit! Publishing and Media Company)

Produced with the assistance of Cheryl Wilson, i4Details and Larry Taylor, LTD2
All rights reserved. No portion of this publication may be reproduced, stored in a retrieval system, or transmitted in any form by any means—electronic, mechanical, photocopy, recording, or otherwise—without the prior written permission of the publisher, except for brief quotations in critical reviews or articles.

All Scripture quotes, unless otherwise indicated, are from the Authorized King James Version of the Bible.

Scripture quotes marked Amplified are from the Amplified Bible, © Copyright 1954, 1958, 1962, 1964, 1965, 1987 by The Lockman Foundation.

Scripture quotes marked NASB are taken from the New American Standard Bible® Copyright © 1960, 1962, 1963, 1968, 1971, 1972, 1973, 1975, 1977, 1995 by The Lockman Foundation.

Scripture quotes marked NIV are taken from the HOLY BIBLE, NEW INTERNATIONAL VERSION®. Copyright© 1973, 1978, 1984 by the International Bible Society.

Scripture quotes marked NLT are taken from the Holy Bible, New Living Translation, copyright © 1996. Used by permission of Tyndale House Publishers, Inc, Wheaton, Illinois 60189. All rights reserved.

Manufactured in the United States of America

www.urbanspirit.biz

MARCH - APRIL - MAY

BUILDING A STRONGER RELATIONSHIP WITH GOD

MARCH
WEEK ONE: FAITH

DAY 1

What is This Thing Called Faith?

STEPPING OUT...

"Now faith is the substance of things hoped for, the evidence of things not seen."

HEBREWS 11:1

"Imani! I haven't seen you in ages," Justine exclaimed from the canned food aisle. She embraced Imani with the grip of a long-lost friend.

"Mommy, who is that?" Justine's six-year-old daughter inquired.

"I'm one of your Mommy's friends from high school," Imani shared. "Can you believe it's been fifteen years, Justine?"

Justine shook her head. "I know. Haven't the years flown by?"

Imani nodded in agreement as she placed a can of tomato paste in the shopping basket. "Well, what are you up to, girl? Where have you been?"

"Actually, I just moved back home. After college I worked my way up the ladder at a computer firm, but they were recently hit hard...."

"I know, this economy is bad right now."

"Yep, so I moved back home. I thought there might be more opportunity here than in a smaller city." They continued down the aisle.

"Not a bad idea," Justine paused and reached for a can of peaches. "Say, Imani, I'm surprised I haven't seen you on the big screen yet. You were dynamic in our school plays and you were always creating productions when we were growing up."

"True, but I've been out of the loop too long. And where do I start?"

"You should go to some auditions. You never know what might happen."

"True," Imani responded reluctantly.

"Pray about it, ask God to order your steps, and step out on faith. You'll be in the right place at the right time," Justine looked down at her watch. "Look, I better run," Justine embraced Imani. "I promise I'll be in touch."

APPLICATION

What is this thing called faith? Hebrews tells us that faith is the substance of things hoped for, the evidence of things not seen. In essence, faith is our most basic need. For Christians, having faith means believing what we can't see because we know God will direct us and supply our needs.

In a rapidly changing world, only one thing is certain—God's promises. At some point in our lives, we have all desired something but you didn't know how it was going to happen. Perhaps your desire was so strong that you made a decision without all the facts. The naysayers claimed you had lost your mind, but you knew it was time because you had faith in God to direct you. You took the risk, left your comfort zone and stepped out in faith.

Today, reflect on promises made to you by others. Then consider the promises in God's Word, the greatest of which is eternal life for those who believe and accept his Son as their personal Savior. When you think of this most precious and perfect gift, how could you not have faith?

PRAYER

Dear Heavenly Father, whose omniscience directs me, I thank you for your most perfect and precious gift, your Son, whom you sent to this world for my salvation. You blessed me with gifts that remain unopened. Sometimes I'm so caught up in my daily comfort zone that I lose sight of my hopes and dreams. They seem distant and unattainable. Lord, I find comfort in knowing your promises are certain. Help me each day to grow in the knowledge that I can trust you as I anticipate the fulfillment of your promises. In Jesus' name. Amen.

DAY 2

Requirements of Faith

HOLDING FAST TO TRUTH...

"But without faith it is impossible to please him: for he that cometh to God must believe that he is, and that he is a rewarder of them that diligently seek him."

HEBREWS 11:6

That night Imani sat in her room and reflected on her life and her dreams. While many viewed acting as a glamorous or risky career, Imani viewed it as an opportunity to change hearts, inspire, and uplift others. Prayerfully, she mapped out a strategy to achieve her dream. After revamping her résumé, taking a photo shoot, and interviewing agents, Imani felt she was ready. She attended some open calls and was elated when she got a callback for an audition.

Each night Justine called Imani to encourage her and pray with her. Justine was as excited about the callback as Imani. She waited anxiously for Imani to arrive at their coffee meeting, certain that Imani would have good news to share.

"So how did the callback go?"

"It went well at first; then they asked me to remove my shirt."

"What?"

"I still want to be an actress, but there are just some things I will not do. I had to decide if I was going to follow the director's instruction to possibly get a role or compromise my values and have faith in God."

"I see God won," Justine replied as she sipped her latté.

APPLICATION

Think back to your youth. You had goals for your personal and professional life that you didn't reach. Perhaps you made all of the preparations—received the degree, completed that training, or made that move—but things didn't work out as you had planned. At first you may have been disappointed, but as you journeyed through life you realized that those goals may not have been God's best for you.

As you think about why your plans didn't come to fruition, ask yourself one very important question. Whose plans are certain, mine or God's? As you contemplate what's next in your life? Consider that God may have you in a holding pattern while He shapes and prepares you for that next step. This is when you most need faith to wait in preparation for the next step God is preparing for you. Remember in all that you do, your desire should be to please God.

PRAYER

Dear Heavenly Father, in your omnipresence I find comfort and security. Thank you for being everywhere at all times preparing the way for me. Lord, I love to be in your presence. I find such peace, joy, and reassurance knowing that you surround me. You've given me free will, but your plan for my life is far better than anything I could imagine. While I don't know what you have planned for me, I have faith that as I strive to uplift your kingdom, you will guide me to the blessing you have in store for me at your appointed hour. In Jesus' name I pray. Amen.

DAY 3

How Much Faith?

HANG IN THERE!

"And Jesus said ... If ye have faith as a grain of mustard seed, ye shall say unto this mountain, Remove hence to yonder place; and it shall remove; and nothing shall be impossible unto you."

MATTHEW 17:20

As the weeks grew into months, Imani began to grow impatient. She had taken on a part-time job to help ends meet while pursuing her acting career. She saw younger actresses win roles, and she wondered if she had missed her opportunity. *"I don't know how much longer I can do this,"* she thought as she drove on the freeway from an audition to her part-time job.

When the melodious notes of a familiar tune began to emanate from the car speakers, Imani turned up the volume. The song provided both instruction and inspiration for her, as the words reminded her that with a modicum of faith, she could perform miraculous feats.

Do you have a mountain in your life that seems impossible to climb? Do you feel that you could do anything if you just had faith? Are you settling for less than God's best because you're weary?

APPLICATION

Today when the storms in life arise, don't despair. Laugh, smile, maintain your positive attitude, and turn those stumbling blocks into stepping stones. Remember that through faith you can meet those challenges. You already have all you need to climb that mountain, realize your dream, or receive God's best for your life: even if your faith is just the size of a mustard seed. You possess all that you need, simply apply that mustard seed of faith to those mountains in your life.

PRAYER

Omnipotent Father, I thank you for the trials you put me through. While they may seem overwhelming, I know that through faith they will be overcome and my faith in you will grow. Remind me, Lord, as I face each test, that I have all the faith I need. In the matchless name of Jesus. Amen.

DAY 4

Enduring in Faith

YOUR ANSWER WILL COME...

"Wherefore seeing we also are compassed about with so great a cloud of witnesses, let us lay aside every weight, and the sin which doth so easily beset us, and let us run with patience the race that is set before us, looking unto Jesus the author and finisher of our faith; who for the joy that was set before him endured the cross, despising the shame, and is set down at the right hand of the throne of God."

HEBREWS 12:1-2

Constant rejections would have broken many a spirit, but Imani viewed them from a different perspective. *"What God has for me is for me,"* she told Justine in reference to her most coveted role. While she was disappointed that she didn't get it, Imani had adopted a "next" attitude. *"If I sit around and dwell on what I didn't get, I'll never be able to move forward."*

"That's right," Justine told her. *"It's not over yet, so don't throw in the towel."* Just as Justine spoke those words, Imani's call waiting signal interrupted their conversation.

"Could you hold on a second, Justine?"

"Sure."

"Guess what?" Imani exclaimed upon returning to Justine.

"I got a part!" she blurted out before Justine could respond.

APPLICATION

Today, as you reflect on your life, remember that whenever you feel overwhelmed by difficulty and disappointment, remember that faith in Christ can sustain you. It's not how fast you run the race, it's important to keep going till you reach the finish line.

PRAYER

Dear omnipotent God, thank you for your Word. In it, you provide us with all the answers to our questions. I trust you, Lord, to guide me in this journey called life. Sometimes the trials I face seem insurmountable; I feel as if I'm stuck in my current position and things will never change. But you are the author and finisher of my faith, and I rest assured that nothing is over until you say it is over. This is my prayer, in Jesus' name. Amen.

DAY 5
Conquerors in Faith

WALK ON...

*"Being confident of this very thing,
that he which hath
begun a good work in you will perform it
until the day of Jesus Christ."*

PHILIPPIANS 1:6

All along, Imani longed just to get her foot in the door. She prayed, along with Justine, for the opportunity to use her talents to uplift God's kingdom. Finally, she landed a role in a film that was consistent with her values and beliefs. During her first day on the set, Imani learned that getting the role was much easier than the demands that would follow.

"Being confident of this very thing, that he which hath begun a good work in you will perform it until the day of Jesus Christ."

PHILIPPIANS 1:6

She had persisted, endured, and expended a great deal of energy in the process. At times she felt as if she wouldn't make it, but just as the Lord had led and sustained her through her search for a role, Imani knew that through Him she would complete it.

APPLICATION

Have you started a project that you're finding difficult to complete? What talents and gifts have you kept to yourself, afraid to share them with the world? Reflect on the past year. Does unfinished business plague you? What is keeping you from completing it? Don't let your fear stand in your way.

As you embark upon your journey and times get rough, just remember that God has blessed you with your talents, skills, and experiences. He will complete the good work he began in you.

PRAYER

Dear omniscient Father, Creator of all things, thank you for the blessing of my gifts and talents. I desire to use them to uplift your kingdom, but sometimes the demands of life make me weary and I wonder if I can run the next mile. Lord, strengthen me and help me take the next step. I know that you have blessed me with these talents, not just for me, but to share with others. Remind me that you finish what you start and that in your timing, you will complete the good work you have begun in me. In Jesus' name, Amen.

BUILDING A STRONGER RELATIONSHIP WITH GOD

MARCH
WEEK TWO: TRUST

DAY 1
Trust During Trials

TRUSTING GOD IS MORE THAN WORDS TO A SONG...

"Woman, why weepest thou? whom seekest thou?"

JOHN 20:15

Deidra prayed about the same problems time and time again. Yet still, her trials and tribulations seemed to mount, and she often cried herself to sleep at night. She told her closest friends how frustrated she was because it seemed God didn't hear her petitions. One of those friends, Sandy, was also her Sunday school group leader.

One Sunday, Sandy ended the lesson by playing a song from a CD. Deidra was surprised because she had the same CD, but she had never listened to that particular song. The song asked a riveting question: What happens to your faith when life is extremely hard? The song brought tears to many eyes in the class, including hers. The words to the song moved and inspired Deidra. She also knew that trusting God was more than simply being moved by the words of a song. Trusting God during trials in life meant work; it meant truly believing God and trusting Him over and above her fears.

APPLICATION

God shields those who trust Him. When life takes us on a detour, God still loves us, protects us, and guides us. Trials will strengthen us if we allow them. James 1:2 says, *"Count it all joy when you fall into various trials"* (NIV). It may be hard to take that view at first. But if we allow the Holy Spirit to lead us, our trials will become triumphs.

The more time we spend in the Word, the more we love it and the more it will fill our minds and hearts. Then when trials come, our minds will be filled with the promises of God, and our faith will be stronger. Get in the habit of studying the Word first thing every morning and see how your days will become easier.

When you read the Word, pray that the Holy Spirit will open your mind to understand what you read so that you will do God's will. Always remember Luke 1:37, "For with God nothing shall be impossible."

PRAYER

Lord, help me to rejoice in knowing that you are using these trials to strengthen my faith. Help me to remember that nothing is impossible with you. Open my eyes to your direction. Lord, remove my fear of the unknown, and open my life to your power today. Work mightily in me! Amen.

DAY 2

Trust in Doubt

WHEN IN DOUBT, HE WILL WORK IT OUT

*"For verily I say unto you,
That whosoever shall say unto this mountain,
Be thou removed, and be thou cast into the sea;
and shall not doubt in his heart,
but shall believe that those things which he saith
shall come to pass; he shall have whatsoever he saith."*

MARK 11:23

A successful television news reporter named Joslyn often attributed her talent and success to pure luck and her hard work. A Christian friend told her that it was more than luck: it was God's grace and blessing that made her successful. Joslyn made it clear to her

colleague that she had worked hard to achieve her level of success, and she had been lucky…period. She didn't see herself as a religious person, and she wasn't interested in hearing more from her Christian colleague.

When problems arose for Joslyn, however, things changed. When her ratings went down, she lost her primetime slot. She started having physical problems, including depression. After a few months, she confided in her Christian coworker that she had made a life-changing decision: she had gone to God for help. Joslyn said that she had prayed to God on her knees. She asked God to forgive her doubt and denial. In time, Joslyn said, she could feel God working with her…changing her.

As her Christian colleague wiped the tears of joy from her eyes, she said, "Joslyn, all things are possible through Christ Jesus. You can rest assured that if God sends you to it, He will see you through it!" They shared a joyous and tearful embrace.

APPLICATION

One of the hardest lessons we will ever learn is to trust God. The human tendency is to lean on our own understanding. But Jesus taught his disciples that if they asked God for something and believed without doubting, they would receive what they ask for. As disciples of Christ, this applies to us as well. When we truly trust God, doors will open that we never even knew existed. *"Call unto me, and I will answer thee, and shew thee great and mighty things, which thou knowest not"* (Jeremiah 33:3).

Start keeping a devotional prayer journal. When facing the unknown, or plagued by insecurities, and doubts, get into the habit of record scriptures, prayers, and blessings. When doubts come to mind, give them to God to deal with. Get on your knees daily and God will hear you out.

PRAYER

Almighty God, I pray that you will take away my doubts. I know you are not the author of confusion. Lord, help me not to doubt you, nor fear what lies ahead. You are a gracious, loving, and merciful savior. Thank you for your grace. Thank you for your love. Please continue to bless, protect, and direct me. Please keep me in your loving care. Amen.

DAY 3

Trust in Healing

WHEN DOCTORS DON'T HAVE AN ANSWER

"Pray for one another, that you may be healed. The effectual fervent prayer of a righteous man availeth much."

JAMES 5:16

Joyce prayed for her sister Christine daily for about a year. She asked the Lord to make a way for Christine and her husband to have a second child. Their first child was six years old and Christine was almost 41. The doctors only gave Christine a 12% chance of becoming pregnant, but they could not foresee God's plan. Christine became pregnant and delivered a healthy baby girl.

Joyce also prayed to God to heal her Aunt Carol, who had been diagnosed with breast cancer. Joyce was a nurse, so she knew that African-American women are disproportionately affected by breast cancer. Thank God, when her aunt went for a second opinion, no cancer was no found. One year later a mammogram and ultrasound detected nothing. Joyce was sure that God had miraculously answered her prayers for Carol and Christine. Praise the Lord!

More than once, Jesus taught about bringing our needs to God, and never giving up; we can keep on asking, seeking, and knocking until God answers. Luke 11:9 says, "And I say unto you, Ask and it shall be given you; seek, and ye shall find; knock, and it shall be opened unto you." We find a similar verse in Matthew 7:8, "For every one that asketh receiveth; and he that seeketh findeth; and to him that knocketh it shall be opened." What encouragement this is! There are numerous examples of God's healing power throughout the Bible. There are also numerous references to God using illness to glorify himself. Either way, Jesus encourages us to ask.

APPLICATION

James assures us that "fervent prayer availeth much." And Hebrews says, "Now faith is the substance of things hoped for, the evidence of things not seen" (11:1). If you have a prayer partner, or go to a Sunday school class or Bible study, share your prayer requests. The power of prayer is awesome. Whether your prayers are for yourself or someone else, being "prayed up" gives you a sense of peace. Prayer changes things.

Make your prayers specific and sincere. When you pray, ask for *God's* will to be done, not yours.

PRAYER

Thank you, Lord, for being Doctor Jesus. When the human doctors can't find the right advice or make the correct diagnosis, thank you for being there. Please guide us in accordance with your will for our lives. Thank you for blessing my family, friends, and me. I trust in your holy name now and forever. Amen.

DAY 4

Trust in Need

God Knows What to Provide before We Know the Need

"We know not what we should pray for as we ought: but the Spirit itself maketh intercession for us with groanings which cannot be uttered."

ROMANS 8:26

Sharon worked for years as a writer for her hometown newspaper. She had an internship during her senior year of college, and then the paper hired her after graduation. After 13 years of working there (and a husband and two children), she had a sincere desire to do

something different. More than anything, Sharon felt the need to be on her own. She felt the need to have more flexibility with her family. Her husband's demanding job didn't allow him much time for family responsibilities. She knew her children needed more parent time.

After much prayer and planning, Sharon stepped out on faith to become a freelance writer. During her years of working in the community, she had made many contacts. But never in her wildest dreams did she think she would be so successful. God had a plan for Sharon that she could not see at first. She just trusted God to make a way out of no way, and he came through. She built a client base and was able to juggle her work schedule and family schedule to make it all work. It wasn't easy, but God gave her what she needed and more.

The Lord's prayer teaches us that it is always right to pray that God be glorified, that his will be done, that our needs be met, and that we be kept from evil (Matthew 6:9-13). The words to the song, *Great Is Thy Faithfulness*, speak beautifully on the same theme. One line says, "All I have needed, thy hand hath provided."

It's truly amazing when you try to comprehend that the Lord knows our needs before we have knowledge of them. Philippians 4:19 says, "But my God shall supply all your need according to his riches in glory by Christ Jesus." It is made as clear as possible for us to understand. But giving up our control and trusting God to supply our needs is hard for us.

God wants to be involved in the everyday details of our lives. He wants us to come to him with everything we need. He loves us and demonstrates his love by supplying our every need.

APPLICATION

When you have needs that you know you can't handle alone, go to God in prayer. If you need confirmation of God's greatness, look to the Word. Do the necessary work required to make changes that need to be made. Ask God to weigh your wants against your needs and choose wisely to follow where he leads. But, trust that God will supply needs beyond your control. Trust that your life can change in ways you haven't even imagined.

PRAYER

Heavenly Father, your Word says you know what I need before I even ask you. In my humble mind, that's hard for me to understand sometimes. Lord, I trust you to supply all my needs. Please help me to truly understand that the more I make myself dependent on you, the better I'll be. I pray that you will empower me to take the steps I need to take as I receive direction from you. Lord, I don't know what's best for me, but I trust your Holy Spirit will guide me. Thank you, Jesus, for showing me how you can make a way out of no way—over and over again. Today, I will trust in your righteousness and rely on your goodness and mercy. In your name I pray, Amen.

DAY 5

Trust in a Blessing

GOD BLESSES US IN SPITE OF US

"And I will make them and the places around about my hill a blessing; and I will cause the shower to come down in his season; there shall be showers of blessing."

EZEKIEL 34:26

Deborah was raised in the church and grew up believing she was a Christian. In college, she got involved with a guy who was the campus drug dealer. She got caught up in that life and made a lot of bad decisions in the name of love.

Eventually, Deborah became a drug carrier for her boyfriend and was arrested on a drug possession charge. During her time in jail, she attended a Bible study session offered by a local church. She remembered her Christian roots and regretted her bad decisions. She realized that she had come to worship her boyfriend and the things he could provide. Now she realized that worshiping Jesus Christ as her Lord and Savior was the only way to go. She prayed to God for forgiveness, and asked him to bless her in spite of her mistakes.

God gave Deborah an opportunity to change, and she made a complete turn around. She knew God had been patient with her, and she was thrilled to have another chance to make her life successful.

A blessing is the gift of God's grace. God blesses us in spite of ourselves. If his grace and mercy came with a dollar figure we could never afford it. We don't earn it. He gives it to us of his own free will. There is nothing on earth more valuable than blessings from above.

APPLICATION

Our spiritual growth and productivity depend on how we hear and receive God's Word into our hearts. Hearing and responding to God's Word brings the blessings of God into our lives.

One way in which you can reach out to share God's blessing with others is by doing prison ministry work. Find a church involved with such a project or start your own. Go to one of the numerous other groups in your city that need volunteer help, or to a group that reaches out to girls. There are many opportunities to be a blessing to others. Ask God to guide you.

PRAYER

Father God, help me balance prayer as a way of thinking versus prayers of requests and crises. Lord, thank you for the many blessings you have bestowed upon me. Help me focus not on selfish desires but on your kingdom work. Thank you for giving me another day to share my blessings with others. Help me to see that you are the greatest blessing of all in my life. Please guide me, heavenly Father. Use me in a way that will change lives and bring souls to you. I give you all the glory, Lord. Amen.

BUILDING A STRONGER RELATIONSHIP WITH GOD

MARCH
WEEK THREE: PRAYER

Alice D. Barrymore

DAY 1
Tired of Talking

WHEN NO ONE SEEMS TO BE ON THE LINE...

"Thou knowest my downsitting and mine uprising, thou understandest my thought afar off. Thou compassest my path and my lying down, and art acquainted with all my ways. For there is not a word in my tongue, but, lo, O Lord, thou knowest it altogether."

PSALM 139:2-4

When Marcia called her girlfriend Nicole, the call went straight to voicemail. It was the third time that she had called Nicole with no answer. Her frustration was rising by the moment. It was the middle of the afternoon.

How could she not answer the phone? Frustrated, Marcia punched in Nicole's number one more time. Come on, answer, she thought to herself. I need you. I need to talk, NOW! Still no answer. Where is a friend when you need one?

APPLICATION

Often, we seek answers to life's pressing problems by turning to a friend, loved one, or neighbor. We depend on others to give meaning to our lives. Or, we look for affirmation and spiritual guidance from prayer partners and pew members alike. When we reach the figurative end of our rope and have exhausted all of our resources, we search the landscape of our lives for a kind word, a gentle embrace, and some genuine counsel and understanding. This is not a bad thing. Scripture tells us it's beneficial to consult others to gain various perspectives (see Proverbs 19:20). There is wisdom in a multitude of counsel. However, the fact is people fail us; they shut down or shut us out, not because they are mean-spirited or evil but simply because they have their own lives and their own issues.

Sometimes we may wonder if God is tired of listening to us, too. We wonder if prayer really works, or is it just an empty ritual. We imagine that God has a caller ID service and all of our calls are being ignored. So, we stop all prayers, both of intercession and thanksgiving.

When you feel that God isn't listening, It's okay to stop talking. Trust that God sees your heart's desire to know him and to be known by him. Believe that he knows your requests before you speak them. Today, change the way you pray. Instead of murmuring and mumbling, write your prayers in a journal or draw a picture, and wait patiently for God's response.

PRAYER

Lord God, when I get tired of talking to you, please talk to me.

When I get weary of worship, please hear the unspoken cries of my heart.

When I faint in our fellowship, forgive my lack of commitment.

I desire to know you and to be known by you.

Help me to hear from you.

In Jesus' name, Amen.

DAY 2
When the need is great

SOME PRAYERS NEED A BOOST...

"This kind can come forth by nothing but prayer and fasting."

MARK 9:29

It was day twenty-one of the church-wide call to prayer. The pastor had proclaimed a time of reclamation and consecration for the everyone. Jean, a leader in the Sunday school department, had committed to daily prayer. Morning, noon, and night she prayed and called out to God. She trusted and believed God for the supernatural and the miraculous. Her knees were marked by the pattern of her bedroom carpet. Her faith and obedience were unquestioned and unparalleled.

But nothing changed, and there was only 10 days left before the end of her commitment. What do you do when prayer is not enough?

APPLICATION

Sometimes the change we long for only comes when we connect fasting and prayer. Fasting can provide a turbo boost to intercession. Abstaining from food for a spiritual purpose can oftentimes catapult prayer beyond the barriers of doubt, dismay and complacency. Fasting aligns us to the power of the supernatural and unleashes the floodgates of the divine. Fasting is a testimony to our hope in God; it shows God that we recognize our need of his provision. Fasting is a radical realignment of priorities that demonstrates our willingness to do God's will while we feast on his word.

Whatever your spiritual needs, fasting will be helpful, if not essential, for your deliverance. Consider taking these steps:

1. Agree with the Word that some challenges are only overcome with prayer and fasting.
2. Choose what kind of fast you will observe: normal (beverages but no solid food), absolute (nothing except water), partial (refrain from a particular food or item), or special (as led by God).
3. Abstain from worldly pleasures and distractions.
4. Pray during the times when you would normally eat.
5. Expect God to answer and move. Anticipate the desired outcome.

6. Stick to your commitment.

7. Thank and praise God in advance and afterward.

PRAYER

Lord, I have done all I know to do. Now I choose to be vulnerable before you. Please honor my sacrifice. Purify my motives and perfect my character. Allow me to see myself as you see me. Cause me to trust and depend on you for everything. I want all that is not like you to be removed from me. In Jesus' name, Amen.

DAY 3

In need of refreshment

ALL ALONE...

*"And when he [Jesus] had sent the multitudes away,
he went up into a mountain apart to pray:
and when the evening was come,
he was there alone."*

MATTHEW 14:23

The conference was over-It was a success! The church was empty, the signs and banners were taken down, the pastors and conference attendee were all headed back to their respective homes. Everyone was exhausted and ready to go home. Debra and her team had done it.

Debra was the lead coordinator, for 3 days, she coordinated a group of 75 volunteers, made sure

all the guest speakers were attended to, and made sure that everything was running smoothly. She had done her part and was tired, weary, and worn. Now that the conference was over, it was time to rest.

APPLICATION

Jesus understood the need to rest and to be alone. Often, after performing a miracle or after a major confrontation with evil, he created space to be alone. He dismissed the crowds and the laborers and went to a secluded place to pray.

Prayer is a time to be reminded of God's concern for your personhood, not just your production. It is a time to be still and become aware of God's intent toward us. Having a consistent prayer life gives you time to pause from life's cares and to attend to what is most important—refreshing your soul and spirit in order to receive instruction from God to do the work of the kingdom.

The challenge of the Christian journey is to know how and when to stop serving and to begin seeking God in prayer. The goal of prayer is not to provide God with your "to do" list, but to intentionally create a time in which we examine our hearts and become aware of what God wants to do in our lives.

Before you start each day, set aside a few moments (at least ten minutes) to simply sit in the presence of God and pray. If your day is as crammed (as for most women), you may have to seize a moment when you can. Get up a few minutes earlier, use your alone time in the car on the way to work, or spend a few extra minutes in the car before entering the building for work.

PRAYER

Lord, sometimes I get so busy serving you that I don't make time to be with you. I pray with others, but don't get around to spending time alone with you. Help me to guard our time together. Help me to keep my date with you. In Jesus' name, Amen.

DAY 4
Honest to God

Praying Your Heart...

"And she [Hannah] was in bitterness of soul, and prayed unto the Lord, and wept sore."

I SAMUEL 1:10

The police were at her front door again. What NOW?! So familiar was their presence in her apartment complex she was certain her family was the main source of gossip in the subdivision. What had her son done now? How much more would she and her husband take? Tears welled up in eyes as she opened the front door. Her heart hurt. Life was not supposed to be this way.

APPLICATION

Often life seems unfair and unjust. We feel defeated and our spirits are sad. In this "name and claim it," I'm blessed and highly favored" Christian culture honestly expressing upset or disappointment is often seen as less spiritual or even sinful. Even though we are taught to pray and trust God for his provision in the midst of our trouble, trusting him does not mean that we refuse to face reality and admit our pain and heartache. We are called not to deny our pain, but rather we are invited to share our concerns with the Lord.

The Bible is full of examples of people who cried out their lament to God from their places of brokenness and disappointment. We need to recover the power of this honest communication with God. Prayer is not just about thanking God in the good times. It is also being honest and real before a caring, attentive God and believing that he can and will answer prayer.

Today, don't hide your feelings from God. Be honest (with yourself) and tell God what is really going on inside you. God is big enough to handle it. If you are uncomfortable saying negative things in your prayer, pray the words of one of the psalms, such as found in Psalm 42 or 69.

PRAYER

Lord, I know that you are able to interpret the moans of my heart. Help me to avoid putting on a false face before I come into your presence. Help me to call out to you even when words fail me and my heart is heavy. I trust that you hear me. I believe that you care. Hear my prayers. In Jesus' name, Amen.

DAY 5

When to Stop

WHAT MAKES PRAYER A WAY OF LIFE…

"Pray without ceasing."
1 THESSALONIANS 5:17

Dorothy grew up in the church. Most Sundays, and many week nights, were spent sitting in the pew. She knew the traditions, teachings, and protocol of the church. She'd served on auxiliaries and committees. She was faithful, dedicated and dutiful. Few could question her commitment to God or the ministry. Her lifestyle was a stellar witness to God's transforming power.

"Pray without ceasing."
1 THESSALONIANS 5:17

It was no major surprise, then, when she was asked to serve on an intercessory team. She went to the first few meetings, only to be overwhelmed by the expectation of its members. Who could pray day and night and on the weekends? When was she to have a life? When was enough, enough?

APPLICATION

When have we prayed enough? Prayer is not only private petition, or corporate intercession; nor is it restricted to certain days, or hours, or seasons; it can be unceasing. Prayer is more than words. It is a way of life that begins at salvation.

Let your life be a prayer—God knows our thoughts and our needs before we pray. We don't have to repeat our concerns over and over to him. When we come to him in prayer, we remind ourselves that he is in control, and we affirm our faith in God's ability to answer our prayers.

Pray with your eyes open, or with your eyes shut. Pray on bended knee, or while standing tall. Pray in the car or on the bus. Pray in the morning, afternoon, or evening. Pray in church; pray at work; pray at home. When have we prayed enough? Never.

PRAYER

Lord, teach me to pray. In Jesus' Name. Amen.

BUILDING A STRONGER RELATIONSHIP WITH GOD

MARCH
WEEK FOUR: MIRACLES

Marjorie L. Kimbrough

DAY 1

The Miracle of Sight

Mama, I Can See across the Street!

"For the Father loveth the Son, and sheweth him all things that himself doeth; and he will shew him greater works than these, that ye may marvel."
JOHN 5:20

During a routine physical at the age of seven it was determined that my older son needed glasses. I took him to an ophthalmologist, and he was fitted for glasses. The morning after he got his glasses, he walked outside and announced in total surprise, "Mom, I can see across the street!"

He did not know that most people could see across the street without glasses, and I felt so guilty for not having known that my son could not see that well.

Wearing glasses has been second nature to him for twenty-seven years now, but he was becoming increasingly concerned that his eyes were steadily deteriorating. He decided to have laser vision correction. During this procedure, pulses of light emitted from the laser surgically reshape the surface of the cornea using the same principles that eyeglasses and contact lenses use.

My son's surgery was quite successful. He was able to see without his glasses immediately following the procedure, and the morning following the surgery he drove himself to the doctor for a checkup. The doctor was amazed by the amount of healing that had already taken place within 24 hours when just the day before he could not see well enough to drive around the corner.

APPLICATION

It is simply amazing to consider how God has designed our eyes and vision. And, it's even more amazing that man has developed the intelligence to mimic what God has done throughout creation. For God this process is natural; for man it is a miracle!

The medical miracle was greater than he had dared to imagine! And that was just what Jesus promised when he told us that God would show us works so great that we would be astonished.

Thank God that you can see this book and read its inspirational words.

PRAYER

Lord, thank you for the intelligence that allows men and women to scratch the surface of your miraculous design of the human body. Amen.

DAY 2

The Final Miracle

I WANT TO BE READY!

*"And if I go and prepare a place for you,
I will come again, and receive you unto myself;
that where I am, there ye may be also."*

JOHN 14:3

My 92-year-old aunt lived a full and active life, but her last days were plagued with health problems. She had diabetes, kidney failure, heart failure, and pneumonia. Her breathing was labored, and her glands were swollen to the point that it was difficult for her to swallow. Yet, my relatives wanted her to hang on. They begged the doctors to use extraordinary measures to prolong her life. They were unwilling to let her go.

As Christians, we need not worry about the dispensation of our earthly vessels because for those who have received salvation the miracle of eternal life is a guarantee. When we have lived our lives in the knowledge of God and have accepted the salvation offered by our Savior, we ought to rejoice when it is time for our final miracle—eternal life. What a blessing it is to let go, to give up this earthly dwelling, and to be welcomed into the arms of the Savior. This is indeed the final miracle, the blessing of all blessings, the glorious gift of eternal life.

APPLICATION

Our earthly bodies will wear out. They become fragile; they function less efficiently, and we find it more difficult to do the things we used to do with ease. Yet, no matter how much our physical bodies deteriorate, we Christians have hope.

Celebrate the life of loved ones who have received the final miracle. Thank God for their life spent here on earth as a testament to God's goodness. Try to do something today that you know would bring joy to their heart.

PRAYER

Lord, thank you for the gift of eternal life. Make us ready to receive our final miracle. Amen.

DAY 3

The Miracle of Friends

WHAT KIND OF FRIENDS DO YOU HAVE?

*"Greater love hath no man than this,
that a man lay down his life for his friends."*

JOHN 15:13

A group of teenage friends living in Orlando, Florida decided to go floating on boogie boards one Saturday in Little Lake Conway. These friends had floated together many times in the past, and they had no reason to believe that this time would be any different. What they didn't know was that there were alligators in the lake now.

Fourteen-year-old Tamika felt something grab her arm. She thought that one of her friends was playing with her until she was being spun around and around. When she realized that an alligator had her in a death spin, she screamed and screamed while trying to pry the alligator's mouth open so that she could remove her arm. Most of her friends swam quickly to shore so that they could get help, but one friend, 14-year-old Amanda, refused to desert Tamika. By this time Tamika believed that she would surely die. She felt her arm snap as the alligator pulled her under the water, and she knew that she would drown and be eaten by the alligator. She thought that this was the way that God had intended for her to die.

However, Amanda had a different view; she knew that she could not leave her friend. She never would have been able to live with her guilt if anything had happened to her friend. Discovering that Tamika couldn't swim with her broken and badly damaged arm, Amanda still managed to get her to shore.

The other friends on shore had gotten help, and Tamika was rushed to the hospital where she received treatment for a broken arm. Amanda was willing to lay down her life for her friend, and God empowered her to save that friend. It was indeed a miracle of friendship.

APPLICATION

Choose someone to whom you can show an act of true friendship today.

PRAYER

Lord, give me the heart of a friend. I want you to use me to save others. Amen.

DAY 4

The Miracle of Assistance

Who Is Running the Peachtree Road Race?

"Wherefore seeing we also are compassed about with so great a cloud of witnesses, let us lay aside every weight and the sin which doth so easily beset us, and let us run with patience the race that is set before us."

HEBREWS 12:1

Every year on the Fourth of July Atlanta clears it famous Peachtree Road for the Peachtree Road Race. It is a 6.2-mile race with over 55,000 participants. While there are both runners and walkers in the crowd, everyone tries to cross the finish line and win the coveted T-shirt.

In one recent race there was a participant who suffered a nearly fatal heart attack during the fifth mile of the race. Although Don had run in the race in years past with no problem, this time he collapsed right in the midst of other runners and walkers. Just then another runner, who saw Don go down, stopped and begin CPR. Then another runner who was a doctor stopped to help. And yet another runner stopped to lead the gathered crowd in prayer. Any of these people could have kept running, but God directed them to the place where they were needed.

Although Don did not remember falling or the CPR that was administered, but he did remember waking up in the ambulance accompanied by the doctor. He was grateful that others were present to help.

APPLICATION

Don was convinced that his survival was a miracle from God. God used everyone he needed to make the miracle a reality. He knows that God miraculously saved him and he hopes to spend this time wisely.

Consider how God wants to use you in each situation in which you find yourself. No matter the situation, you can be used by God.

PRAYER

Lord, thank you for your angels who are with us to help us finish the race. Amen.

DAY 5

The Miracle of Answered prayer

Do You Really Believe in Answered Prayer?

"Therefore I say to you, What things so ever ye desire, when ye pray, believe that ye receive them, and ye shall have them."

MARK 11:24

The downturn in the economy had been so hard for one family that they were not sure how they would make ends meet. Both the father and the mother had lost their jobs due to downsizing, the baby was sick and needed expensive medicine, and the rental house in which they lived had been sold. So, on top of everything else, they had to move. All the family could do was pray, and pray they did.

There is something unusual about sincere and fervent prayer. It inspires those praying to get up off their knees and hustle. After the prayer, the father and mother started talking about the various courses of action open to them. They thought about trying to become apartment managers so that they would have a place to live with free or reduced rent. They talked about asking the owner of the grocery store where they shopped to extend their credit until they had some income, but they had no solution for the expensive medicine their baby needed.

While they were reviewing their situation, they received a phone call from a friend who told them of an apartment building that desperately needed a manager. They immediately made an appointment to meet the owner and were hired. They explained their cash flow situation, and the owner said that in addition to the apartment building, he also owned a store in which the father could work extra hours. The family was overjoyed and grateful to God, but they still needed the baby's medicine. So the father explained the baby's needs and asked for a cash advance. To his great surprise he discovered that the owner's store was a pharmacy, and the owner said that he would be happy to run a tab for them so that they could get the medicine they needed. It was an answer to their prayers. God had supplied all their needs.

APPLICATION

Pray with faith, believing that your prayers will be answered. Do it today!

PRAYER

Lord, you are always working to provide for your children. Help us to become your agents, offering assistance to those in need and witnessing to your love. Amen.

UNDERSTANDING THE CROSS

April
WEEK ONE:

Day 1
He is Who He is

WE CAN KNOW HE IS REAL...

"The woman saith unto him, I know that Messias cometh, which is called Christ: when he is come, he will tell us all things. Jesus saith unto her, I that speak unto thee am he."

JOHN 4:25,26

A woman had grown up believing that God was watching, but from a distance. She believed that when God was done creating, he just sat back and watched what he created. She could never understand that God could be a participant in a world full of sin and deprivation. She found no evidence that Jesus was anybody but a good person who had delusions of grandeur. After all, he thought he was God. *Gee,* she thought, *if he were alive today, they'd be locking him up for perpetrating a fraud, or he'd be in a straitjacket.*

APPLICATION

The entire foundation of Christianity is built upon the fact that Jesus is the Messiah written about by the ancient prophets. Thus, If the resurrection actually happened, then Jesus is who he said he is. No matter what man does, God is able. Nothing and no one can prevent what God wills. So, the next morning, the almost two-ton stone had been rolled away—and Jesus was gone.

If you really want to know that Jesus is real then think about what your life was like without him. Write down some of the things that he has done for you. More importantly, start keeping a journal and write down where you are today. Next week, next month, next year you'll be at another level of faith and glory in Christ.

PRAYER

Dear Lord, I want to know you better. I want to know who you truly are in my life. I surrender myself to die to this world and to be resurrected with you. Lord, thank you for not coming into this world to condemn me as a sinner, but to save me from my sin. Thank you that salvation does not depend on my desire or effort, but on God's mercy. Jesus, I not only acknowledge you as my Savior, but as Lord of my life now and forever more. Amen.

Day 2

Oh Happy Day

Nothing but the Blood of Jesus...

"For the life of the flesh is in the blood: and I have given it to you upon the altar to make an atonement for your souls: for it is the blood that maketh an atonement for the soul."

LEVITICUS 17:11

A young woman had all that the world had to offer. She had a good job, good friends, plenty of money, and was fine looking to boot. She also accepted all of the ways of the world. From her standpoint she had a lot of living to do, and none of it was going to pass her by. She worked hard all week, and when the weekend came she played equally hard. Men came in and out of her life, not by design, but because she was in the process of looking for the right one. She enjoyed the process, and if the right one never came along, that was okay, too. Interviewing candidates was becoming more fun anyway, she thought. She was sexually active, but she did not consider herself promiscuous. She got to know each man and never became intimate with any of them until at least the third date.

Oh yes, she was a Christian. She accepted Christ as a teenager. She believed what the Bible said, but believed that some of it, like the part about sex, really wasn't applicable for today's living. Let's keep it real. No man is going to get serious, let alone marry a woman whom he hasn't had sex with.

APPLICATION

Isn't it funny how we cherry pick the scriptures to find support for our personal agendas? Or, how we decide that certain bible verses are no longer relevant (and there are some) because they are out dated or don't fit into our personal opinion or interpretation? Well, the fact is most people cherry pick the Bible--it's ok. However, what's not ok is to cherry pick scripture simply to justify sin. Jesus shed His blood as atonement for our sin (see 1 John 2). He laid down his life such that our life might be transformed. Scripture says that ALL have sinned and fall short of the glory of God (Romans 3:23). But Christ is our Redeemer, He doesn't want any to perish under the weight of their own sin.

Take a small piece of white cloth and put a red stain on it. Carry the white cloth in your pocket or in your purse as a keepsake. Every time you see it, remember that it is the blood of Jesus that saved us and cleansed us that we might come into the presence of the Father. Make it a habit to pray the blood of Jesus over every person and every situation you encounter, especially those that lead you into sin.

PRAYER

Lord, I thank you that you continue to intercede for me at the right hand of the Father. I thank you for the power you have given my life through the blood of Jesus. I thank you that you have chosen me to know your will and to see the Righteous One and to hear words from his mouth as you said in your Word.

www.urbanspirit.biz

Day 3
What we Celebrate

WE CELEBRATE GRACE, NOT LEGALISM...

"Let no man therefore judge you in meat, or in drink, or in respect of an holyday, or of the new moon, or of the sabbath days: Which are a shadow of things to come; but the body is of Christ. Let no man beguile you of your reward in a voluntary humility and worshipping of angels, intruding into those things which he hath not seen, vainly puffed up by his fleshly mind."

COLOSSIANS 2:16-18

A teenage girl totally gave her heart to Christ. She was living for Jesus and He was Lord of her life. On Easter she invited some friends from her youth group to her house for dinner

after morning church services. Her parents had an Easter egg hunt for her little brothers and sisters. She noticed that some of the youth group leaders were a little standoffish, not at all enjoying the festivities. Later she offered them some of the candy from the Easter basket that her parents had prepared and they politely, but condescendingly, turned it down. She commented to one of her friends that she thought that she liked jellybeans. Her friend responded, "I do." The girl said, "Well, then, here take them home, I can't stand them." Her friend again declined, saying that the whole thing about Easter baskets and Easter egg hunts is a pagan ritual and that she would rather spend her day worshipping the Lord than participating in such things.

Besides being embarrassed, the young girl began to question her own dedication and relationship with Christ. Maybe she should stop doing these things, she thought, to show genuine love for the Lord on the holiest of all days.

APPLICATION

Are you being judgmental about how others worship the Lord? Are you measuring how much they love the Lord by what they do? For that matter, are you measuring your own love for the Lord by what you do? Christ is in your heart, and how you celebrate him is also in your heart. You could dash away from the dinner table to read Scripture, but be committing a sin because you left the food on the table and dishes for others to clean up after you. You could go to Bible study every week, yet sin because you judge your neighbor who misses every other week. Your judgmental attitude can easily turn into legalism over the way you worship God; you begin to worship the activity itself. Even worse, you begin to take pride in what you have done for the Lord rather than humbling yourself because of what he has done for you.

God ordained specific celebrations and feasts for the people of Israel to enjoy. Jesus himself attended these feasts. Present-day Christian celebrations have grown out of these ancient feasts of Israel. Satan confuses us into thinking that, as Christians, we should not enjoy ourselves. We've got to keep Christ in the center of everything that we do, and enjoy him as the great gift of God that he is.

Next time you are in a group of Christians who are about to participate in an activity that you are not sure is "Christ-centered," go ahead and be a part of it rather than standing back. However, be the one to bring Christ into it: suggest that grace be said at the dinner table just before everyone digs into the food; mention his name in conversation, or just praise his name in the midst of others. You might find that the children mimic you by thanking Jesus for the candy they got, or the fun they had.

PRAYER

Lord, let me be led by the Holy Spirit in all that I do. I pray that you give me wisdom in the way that I act toward others. Help me make the most of every opportunity. Let my conversation be always full of grace, seasoned with salt, so that I may know how to answer everyone (Colossians 4:4-6). In Jesus' name, Amen.

Day 4
Resurrection Appearances

WOULD YOU RECOGNIZE HIM?

"But their eyes were holden that they should not know him. Then he said unto them, O fools, and slow of heart to believe all that the prophets have spoken: Ought not Christ to have suffered these things, and to enter into his glory?"

LUKE 24:16, 25-26

A woman had been orphaned as a child and went from foster home to foster home. The only activity she loved was dancing. When she came of age, she embarked on a dancing career and was able to find steady work in regional dance companies. In her early twenties, she was stricken with a rare form of cancer. Although she survived the cancer, she would never be able to continue her dance career.

That woman thanked the Lord daily for his healing powers. But unfortunately, without dance, she felt lost and without a purpose in life. Daily, she asked the Lord for guidance to show her what purpose he had for her now. God answered her prayer. He showed her that hers was a soul-saving testimony meant to help others reach their dream of having a career in the performing arts. Ten years later, she had built a world-renowned program that supported hundreds in dance, music, and art around the world. She thanked the Lord for her illness because he used her testimony to take as a tool for winning souls to Christ.

APPLICATION

What do you do when life doesn't turn out as you planned? In order to have power and authority in our own lives, we have to have our eyes opened to recognize who Jesus is when he shows up.

Just because things may not be going as you expect them to right now doesn't mean that God is not in the midst. God can use anything or anyone for his glory. Look for Jesus in the people around you. If you recognize Christ in another person, then there will be power in your relationship with them.

PRAYER

Lord, I want to recognize you whenever you show up in my life. I want to see your face, and I want to know your voice. In the mighty name of Jesus. Amen.

Day 5

Lighter than Air

THE ASCENSION

"Humble yourselves in the sight of the Lord, and he shall lift you up."

JAMES 4:10

A male coworker asked a woman if she wouldn't mind taking on a little extra work for him a few weeks while he was out on parental leave after the birth of his first son. The woman told the man that she couldn't because she was too busy her own projects. When in reality, she had the time but she thought the co-worker's job was beneath her. Even though they were both salespeople, he had the least lucrative accounts in the company.

THE NEW WOMEN OF COLOR DAILY DEVOTIONAL

"Humble yourselves in the sight of the Lord, and he shall lift you up."
JAMES 4:10

Later that year the woman took sick for a long period. Without being asked, the man took over her workload, keeping it up to date until she returned from sick leave. Upon her return, she discovered that the man had done such a good job demonstrating that he could manage such a heavy workload, he had acquired two very lucrative accounts that far exceed hers.

APPLICATION

First Peter 5:5, says that God sets himself against the proud, but he shows favor to the humble." To be humble before God in service requires submission and sacrifice. Jesus had to humble himself had to be crucified before he could ascend. Humbling yourself before God means taking the focus off yourself and focusing it on God and what he would have you do. When we humble ourselves, the Lord can elevate us; when we elevate ourselves, we are foolishly saying that we don't need God's help.

PRAYER

Lord, I want to live for you. Whatever you have in mind for me, high society or low person on the totem pole, I humble myself to your will and your way. Give me a chance to work for your glory. In your precious name I pray, Amen.

UNDERSTANDING THE CROSS

APRIL
WEEK TWO: MERCY AND GRACE

DAY 1

God's grace and Mercy Toward Me

OH, BUT FOR YOUR GRACE!

*"And he said,
I will make all my goodness pass before thee,
and I will proclaim the name of the Lord before thee;
and will be gracious to whom I will be gracious,
and will shew mercy on whom I will shew mercy."*

EXODUS 33:19

Sylvia and Meshell, both attractive women in their mid-30s, were enjoying their monthly Saturday luncheon.

"I'm so blessed to have a friend like you," Meshell told Sylvia.

"Remember that God has placed us in each other's lives for a specific reason," Sylvia replied.

Meshell began to reminisce about the many times that Sylvia and her husband took Meshell and the children in after Meshell's husband had gone on drunken rages.

Sylvia smiled sweetly at her friend. "Girl, we did a lot of fasting and praying for you to get out of that situation."

Meshell laughed before she spoke, "And you never stopped praying for me." After a thoughtful pause, Meshell confided again, "It would have been so easy for me to be jealous about how God had chosen to bless you in your life."

"Oh, but for God's grace and mercy towards me, your story could easily have been mine," Sylvia quickly responded.

Both Sylvia and Meshell thanked God for their experiences.

APPLICATION

God will do just what he said he would do. You are where you are for a specific reason. God wants you to live for him. Stop right now and read Exodus 33:19. God has promised to always give us the grace and mercy that we need. Your spiritual growth is important to him. The trials and tribulations that you encounter are to make you stronger. Psalms 103:13 says, *"Like as a father pitieth his children so the Lord pitieth them that fear him."*

Take a piece of paper and draw a line straight down the center. On the left side, write "Problem" and on the right side, write "God's Purpose." Make a list of your problems and then, on the right side, write down what God might want you to learn as a result of your problems. This is a good way to identify your purpose and to chart your spiritual growth. Keep adding to your list on a regular basis.

PRAYER

Dear heavenly Father, I come to you today thanking you for the many experiences that make me stronger and bring me closer to you. Father God, I ask you to continue to pour out your grace and mercy on me. Thank you, Lord. Amen.

DAY 2

*Grace and Mercy Toward
Those Who Use You*

God, Must I Be Kind to this Person?

*"Surely he scorneth the scorners:
but he giveth grace unto the lowly."*

PROVERBS 3:34

Kellie has worked hard to make it to her executive position. She is a born-again Christian who gives God all the praise and honor for her successes and achievements. She's always played by the rules and has never done anything inappropriate to climb the corporate ladder.

After her most recent promotion, several people in Kellie's department stopped speaking to her. In fact, they had even started talking about her behind her back. While riding the elevator one day, Kellie spoke to a lady who had worked in her department for about two years. The lady not only did not respond to Kellie, but she rolled her eyes and walked quickly off the elevator when the doors opened. Kellie got so angry that she told God, "Lord, I not going to keep taking this treatment from people who really don't know me and mean me no good!" Suddenly, Kellie heard a still voice say, "Yes, you will."

The next day the same lady entered the elevator and Kellie spoke to again. "Good Morning," she said. Quickly the lady turned around and shot her a look that could kill, rolled her eyes, and turned back to face the elevator door.

That was it! Kellie asked, "What have I done to you that you don't like me?"

Suddenly, the lady turned around and began to rattle off a list of offenses as if she had been waiting a lifetime to tell Kellie these things. "You think you're all that. You got a promotion and now you act like you better than everyone else. You used to be one of us," she said, "and now you think you got it going on with your fancy car and your fancy new home."

Kellie quickly responded, I thank God each and every day for every blessing that he's given me." After a small breath, Kellie continued, "It's only because of God's grace and mercy (and a lot of hard work) that I've been able to achieve such success. And, I'm not one bit ashamed or remorseful about what I've been able to achieve through Christ. I pray that one day you will experience God's grace (unmerited favor) and mercy (compassion) and then maybe you will understand the goodness of God." With that the elevator doors opened, and Kellie left the elevator.

APPLICATION

Instead of getting mad and responding negatively to her co-worker, Kellie gave God the glory. She realized that God was working through her to demonstrate the love of Christ. Over the next few months, Kellie's co-worker began to watch her and how she interacted with others, how she conducted herself in meetings, and how she treated her peers and her subordinates. Every time she encountered her co-worker in the elevator or in the breakroom, she went out of her way to speak and to be kind to her—to show God's grace and mercy.

Whom do you know who needs to hear about the grace and mercy of God? Make yourself a Word Box. Jot down meaningful Scriptures on 3 x 5 index cards and put them in a box on your desk at work or in a central location in your home. When you, a family member, or a co-worker need a quick word of encouragement or wisdom thumb through the box and select a verse to read.

PRAYER

Thank you, dear Lord, for blessing me. Thank you for your saving grace and your tender mercies. Thank you for honoring my efforts to bless your holy name. Help me to remember to show mercy toward others and to serve others as a good steward of your grace. (1 Peter 1:10)

DAY 3
God's Grace and Mercy Never Runs Out

HE HAS KEPT ME THROUGH IT ALL!

"He is the tower of salvation for his king: and sheweth mercy to his anointed, unto David, and to his seed for evermore."

2 SAMUEL 22:51

LaDona has made some terrible decisions for most of her adult life, including substance abuse. Now, LaDona proclaims Jesus Christ to be her personal Lord and Savior. She told her sponsor, who is a Christian, that she knows that God loves and cares for her.

Her sponsor replied, "You are so right, LaDona. God does love and care for you, and he wants you to love and care for yourself as well."

"I'm so glad that God has never run out of grace and mercy for me," LaDona replied. "I'm glad that he has kept me through all of my sinful ways."

"Yes, that means that God has something for you to do for the uplifting of his kingdom," agreed her sponsor.

"I've been drug free for 6 months now and I can truly feel God's grace upon me. I want this to be the last time that I ask God for his grace and mercy for this situation!"

The sponsor smiled. "Give it to God, LaDona. Give it to God and ask him to abide in your life, and then take it one day at a time."

APPLICATION

It's wonderful to know that God gives us new grace and mercy every day. He doesn't put limitations on his grace and mercy towards us, and neither does he keep a running tally of how many times we need his grace and mercy. Do not hesitate to ask God for his grace or his mercy. No matter what you have done or what situation you may be in, remember that God never runs out of mercy and grace.

Start a Gratitude Journal. God's grace and mercy should motivate you to live a life of gratitude. Now that you have a fresh new day, filled with God's fresh grace and mercy, what has God done for you that you are thankful for? Write it down. What can you do better today than you did yesterday to demonstrate your gratitude for God's grace and mercy toward you? Write it down.

PRAYER

"Withhold not thy tender mercies from me, O Lord: let thy lovingkindness and truth continually preserve me" (Psalm 40:11). Thank you, Father, for your grace and mercy, for giving me the opportunity to get it right, and not judging me when I get it wrong. Amen.

DAY 4

Grace and Mercy that will see you through

I don't Know if I'll Make It Through!

"And therefore will the Lord wait, that he may be gracious unto you, and therefore will he be exalted, that he may have mercy upon you: for the Lord is a God of judgment: blessed are all they that wait for him."

ISAIAH 30:18

Linda believes in God. She believes that Jesus died on the cross to save her soul. She loves worshiping God and working in her church. Linda thanks God daily for her husband, children, family, and friends…but today is different.

Linda called her mother and said, "Mother, I need for you to pray for me right now!"

"What's wrong?" Linda's mother asked.

"Mom, just pray!"

Linda's mother stopped for a quick, frantic prayer, then took a breath before she asked again, "Now, what's wrong?"

In a small voice, Linda said, "Mother, I've just found out that I have breast cancer."

Linda's mother took a moment as she composed herself. "Are you sure?" she asked.

"Yes, I am. I want you to go in with me next week when I hear about my treatment choices."

While waiting for the doctor's appointment, Linda and her entire family went on a fast. Linda's church family also fasted and prayed with her. Linda's mother traveled with her to the appointment where they listened to the options that Linda faced. They prayed and chose together.

Linda had the lump removed and also underwent chemotherapy. That was two years ago. Linda is strong and healthy today. Reminiscing with her mother, Linda said, "Mother I know that it was all of our prayers and God's grace and mercy that brought me through. I almost lost it when I got my results, but I remembered that by God's stripes I could be healed. I remembered all the other storms that God had brought my family through, so I had to believe that he would see me through this one, too."

APPLICATION

God promises to never leave us or forsake us. God promises to never leave us comfortless. We have to have the faith to stand on God's Word. We must have the faith to know that God said it and that settles it. God is fully aware when we are scared, but he is not concerned with the outcome. God is, however, concerned with what we do and how we react in times of trouble and strife. Remember Philippians 4:6-9 and ask God for wisdom. Ask God for the grace and mercy to endure.

Write your problem down on a piece of paper. Fold it up and say a prayer over it. Do not reopen it or throw the paper away. When the problem has been resolved, open it and see how God has worked. Keep these papers and refer back to them when you think that God does not hear your cries. You will see that God has always been there to answer your prayers. The answer you receive may not be the one that you want or the one you expect, but God knows what's best for you. Count it all joy.

PRAYER

Father, when I can't see my way ahead, please remind me that you are in charge of my life. That you will never leave me or forsake me. Remind me that you are commander and chief of this life that I live each day. Oh God, I will give you all the praise and honor and glory. Thank you for dying on the cross. Thank you, God, for caring about me. Amen.

DAY 5

*Accepting God's Grace and
Mercy for your life*

WHAT A HARD THING TO DO!

*"Surely goodness and mercy shall follow me
all the days of my life: and I will dwell
in the house of the Lord forever."*

PSALM 23:6

Cynthia had been feeling depressed and down lately and burdened by the feeling that she didn't feel worthy of God's grace and mercy. She made an appointment to speak with her pastor.

"I just don't feel as if I deserve God's mercy and grace." Cynthia said; "I'm not always the best wife, mother, friend, or Christian that I can be."

The pastor responded, "Cynthia, none of us are worthy of God's grace or mercy. We've all have sinned and fallen short of God's glory (Romans 3:23). The good news is God uses grace and mercy to sustain us! In fact, his grace and mercy toward us are the ultimate expression of his love for us and the reason we're saved. Go home and study Ephesians 2:4-9 and let's talk again soon."

APPLICATION

Receiving God's grace and mercy can be a hard thing to do because sometimes we feel so unworthy. Nobody is perfect. We all have some area of our life that could use some work. However, we must realize that despite our shortcomings and our downfalls, God is merciful. God's grace abounds in the face of our sin (Roman 5:20). God in his grace (unmerited favor), is willing to give us chance after chance to get it right. All we have to do is humble ourselves, confess and repent of our shortcomings.

In your gratitude journal, begin to list out a few of your recent accomplishments. This list is not to puff you up or to gloat in any way. Instead, it will allow you to see how God's grace and mercy has brought you through. It may also help you to realize that even the even the bad things were for your good! Begin to thank God today for his grace and mercy bestowed upon you!

PRAYER

Dear Lord, thank you for raining down your grace and mercy on me. Thank you, dear Lord, for your many, many chances you've given me to get it right. Thank you for not counting my shortcomings against me. Continue to bless me, Lord. Continue to give me the opportunity to bless your holy name. Amen.

UNDERSTANDING THE CROSS

APRIL
WEEK THREE: BOLDNESS

DAY 1

Who Is on the Lord's Side?

ONLY THE STRONG SURVIVE!

"If thou wilt go with me, then I will go: but if thou wilt not go with me, then I will not go."

JUDGES 4:8

In the book of Judges we read how the Israelites did evil in the sight of God and found themselves in trouble time and time again. In chapter 4 it was Jabin the Canaanite king who was tormenting them.

Deborah was a prophetess, a woman of extraordinary wisdom and a respected leader. She was sitting under a palm tree when God spoke to her heart and gave her explicit instructions about what to do with Jabin and his wicked army.

Deborah called Barak, her military leader, and said, "The Lord God of Israel commands you to go. Take ten thousand men to the river Kishon. I will draw Jabin's army with his chariots and multitude; I will deliver them into your hand."

Barak replied to Deborah, "Only if you go with me will I go."

Perhaps Barak was afraid that his strength was not reliable. He wanted the Lord's prophet to go with him.

APPLICATION

Have you ever applied for a job that you knew you weren't 100% qualified for? You read the job description evaluated the qualifications and assessed the duties and responsibilities the position had to offer. You concluded that while you may not possess ALL the qualifications the job demanded, you possessed at least 60% of the skills necessary to get the job done. You prayed about it; your co-workers encouraged you to apply, your friends told you to apply, and you knew in your heart you could do the job. But, in the end, you talked yourself out of applying for the position because you lacked 40% of skills the position you required. Only to find out later that the person they hired in the position had even fewer qualifications than you?

Quit sitting on the sidelines watching life pass you by. Be BOLD! Take a chance! So, what if they tell you NO! How will you ever hear YES if you never try. Today as you pray, ask God for the holy boldness that only he can give. Stop letting the enemy convince you that you can't and watch see that God CAN!

PRAYER

Lord, give me the courage to be bold; to stand with you. Let the boldness of your Holy Spirit strengthen me as I step out in faith on your word. Amen.

DAY 2

Into the Hand of a Woman

PRESSING THE WRONG BUTTON...

"For the Lord shall sell Sisera into the hand of a woman."

JUDGES 4:9

Deborah consented to go with Barak into battle. However, she informed him that he would not receive the honor. The Lord would overthrow Jabin's army and sell Sisera into the hands of a woman. Barak probably thought Deborah was speaking of herself. Little did he know God had another plan.

Barak gathered his ten thousand. Sisera gathered his nine hundred chariots of iron, and his great hosts of men near the river. God led the Israelites down into the valley of the Kishon River. There he sent a mighty rain cloud. The rain began to fall, rivers began to swell, and Jabin's army was discomfited. The sound from the 900 chariots crashing into each other began to make loud noises; those mighty chariots became useless. The rain beating against the iron also became unbearable. Chariots were stuck in the mud everywhere. It caused chaos. There was mass confusion (Judges 4:8-15).

What a mighty God we serve. He saved the Israelites.

APPLICATION

Have you ever sat a computer keyboard, pressed the wrong key, and the file you were working on disappeared? You panic, where did everything go?! In an act of desperation, you reboot the computer hoping, praying that the all your hard work is not lost. As the computer comes back to life, you feel a sense of joy and relief when a message flashes across the monitor that reads, *file recovered*. The Israelites knew that joy a thousand times over because of the many times that God rescued them. We, too, have been rescued—recovered by the cross of Calvary. Just think what God can do with our enemies if we would only seek him first.

God never intended for us to fight our battles alone. Reflect on the number of times God has rescued you from whatever situation you found yourself in? Today present each of your enemies to God in prayer and then watch to see how He will deliver you.

PRAYER

Lord, help me to have the faith of Deborah when I face my enemies. Give me the assurance of knowing that my enemies have already been delivered into your hands.

Amen.

DAY 3
Waiting for the Right Time

Don't Forget to Call Home!

"And the Lord discomfited Sisera and all his chariots and all his host."

JUDGES 4:15

With God's small army and the element of surprise, the Israelites successfully overtook the Canaanite army. Sisera panicked when he looked around and saw his men being utterly defeated. He could not believe his eyes, so he fled on foot.

Barak pursued Sisera's army until there was not a man left. God destroyed the entire army. None were left alive, no more would they taunt the Israelites (Judges 4:15-16).

APPLICATION

Are there times when you feel you can't go any further and you've cried out to God saying, *"How long, Lord, how long? When will it be my turn?"* And then the Holy Spirit provides strength and begins to encourage your heart.

God does not do things half way; he acts with the boldness. When we follow the will of God and carry out his instructions, we, too, can act with boldness.

Write down or tell someone else about a time in your life when you thought that you could not go on, but God responded with his boldness and strength.

PRAYER

Dear Lord, Speak courage to my heart, Lord, and put my enemy on the run. Vanquish my enemy utterly as you did Sisera's army. Amen.

DAY 4
Safety in The Arms of a Woman?

YOU CAN RUN, BUT YOU CAN'T HIDE!

"Sisera fled away on his feet to the tent of Jael the wife of Heber."

JUDGES 4:17-23

Sisera ran as fast as he could from the scene of his army's defeat. He was looking for a safe haven. This sell-out soldier had abandoned his own men. Unfortunately for Sisera, he ran right into the judgment of God.

Sisera ran to the tents of his allies and was invited into the tent of Jael, the wife of his ally.

When she invited him in, Sisera thought he was safe. Since it was not customary for a man to enter into a tent of a woman, Sisera hoped no one would look for him there. To be even more sure, he asked Jael to stand watch at the entrance of the tent and instructed her, *"If anyone comes along and asks if I'm here, say no."* Jael, being a gracious host, took care of Sisera. She gave him some milk and then covered him again with a blanket. Soon Sisera snuggled beneath the covers and fell into a deep sleep thinking he had become invisible to the world and escaped God's judgement; but not so!

APPLICATION

You can't hide from yourself and you certainly can't hide from God. There is an old R & B song by Teddy Pendergrass that says, *"You can't hide from yourself, everywhere you go there you are."* God is the same; he is everywhere you go. Have you ever tried to hide from God? Were you hiding because of sin, or unbelief? Or were you running from something he wanted you to do? Where can we flee from God's presence? There is nowhere we can go. Wherever we go, God is there.

Psalm 139:7-12 tells us there no hiding from God.

> *"Whither shall I go from thy spirit? Or whither shall I flee from thy presence? If I ascend up into heaven, thou art there: if I make my bed in hell, behold, thou art there. If I take the wings of the morning, and dwell in the uttermost parts of the sea; even there shall thy hand lead me, and thy right hand shall hold me. If I say, surely the darkness shall cover me; even the night shall be light about me. Yea, the darkness hideth not from thee; but the night shineth as the day: the darkness and the light are both alike to thee"*

PRAYER

Lord God, I cannot hide from you. No matter where or why I try to hide, yet you know where I am and why I am hiding. Help me, Lord, to never want to hide from you again. Amen.

DAY 5

What's in Your Hand? Use It!

Stand up and Be Counted...

"So God subdued on that day Jabin the king of Canaan before the children of Israel."

JUDGES 4:23

In Palestine it was customary for wives to repair and anchor the huge tents in which they lived, while the men were out making tents and doing other things. When Sisera stumbled toward Jael's tent, he may have loosened one of the nails (or tent pegs) that held the tent in place through winds and storms. These nails were quite long with a very sharp point at the end.

When Jael bent down to repair the tent, perhaps God spoke to her heart, as he did with Moses, "What is in your hand?" (Exodus 4:2). At any rate, we know that Jael took the nail in one hand and the hammer in the other, tiptoed to the sleeping Sisera, and drove the nail through his temple right into the ground.

Barak, still hunting for Sisera, came to the tent. Jael came out to meet him and said, "Come, I will show you the man you are looking for." God's prophecy was fulfilled. The children of Israel prospered and prevailed against Canaan.

Jael's act of bravery helped to set her people free from the oppression of the Canaanites. God gave them rest for forty years. Because of her courageous act, Jael was blessed by Deborah in Judges 5:24.

APPLICATION

Imagine what Jael must have thought as she considered what she was about to do. Lord, do you really want me to skewer this man's skull? What if he woke up? What if her husband, Sisera's ally, got mad at her? Yet the Bible records no doubts. It just states what she did. She carried out the will of God.

When God places you a situation and he needs to count on you, it takes courage to-be bold! Know that God always goes before you! I'm sure if Jael had time to think about what she was about to do; she might not have done it. She was not there when Deborah prophesied concerning the victory. She only acted on the intuition of the Holy Spirit. What courage, obedience and holy boldness that must have taken.

What an example for each of us can live by. Let God order your steps. Is God asking you to do something bold? Something that requires you to step outside of your comfort zone and trust him? Write it down and begin to pray to God to give you hold boldness to tackle the task at hand.

PRAYER

Lord, help me not to question your voice, help me to move when you speak; to step out in boldness and trust that you, Lord, are with me. Teach me to stay in tune to you. Amen.

UNDERSTANDING THE CROSS

APRIL
WEEK FOUR: SALVATION

DAY 1
Salvation for the Asking

THERE IS POWER IN PRAYER...

"Then Eli answered and said, Go in peace: and the God of Israel grant thee thy petition that thou hast asked of him. And she said, Let thine handmaid find grace in thy sight. So the woman went her way, and did eat, and her countenance was no more sad."

1 SAMUEL 1:17-18

During seminary, a friend and I decided to meet a couple of hours before a Greek exam to study. When we began, I said, *"We will begin studying wherever the Bible opens to in the Gospel of John."* It opened to John 5:19 so that is where we began. After studying for one-and-a-half hours we decided to take a break before the exam. We prayed together before we left the room, *"Lord, let the professor have mercy on us in his selection of the Scripture."* We took our break and went to class. When the professor came in, he said, *"Let me see, where shall we begin? How about John 5:19?"* I am no special person with a special portion of faith. God answers prayer.

In 1 Samuel 1:13-18 we read about a very depressed woman, Hannah, and her prayer. Hannah's problem centered on being barren. Conceiving and bearing a male child in the Old Testament was synonymous with finding favor with God—gaining salvation. So it was her relationship with her God about which Hannah was really concerned.

Hannah had a "broken and a contrite heart," and she went to the One who could help her. Hannah asked God, Hannah confessed to God, Hannah received from God, and Hannah obeyed God. I imagine that when God heard Hannah's prayer and saw Hannah's tears, God probably wept.

The prayer of Hannah required something her. It required faith. Faith brought an answer to Hannah's prayer, and faith will bring answers to your prayers. Even your prayers about salvation.

APPLICATION

Commit all your concerns to the Lord, particularly your concern about your salvation. Have faith that the blood of Jesus Christ is sufficient to save you. Pray a prayer of faith and believe God for an answer.

PRAYER

Oh Lord, have mercy upon me. I accept your offer of salvation and I will be forever grateful for the sacrifice your son, Jesus Christ, made to save my soul. Amen.

DAY 2

Salvation—A Change in Direction

YOU NEED A GUIDE...

"Blessed is he whose transgression is forgiven, whose sin is covered. Blessed is the man unto whom the Lord imputeth not iniquity, and in whose spirit there is no guile."

PSALM 32:1-2

A woman dressed in a cheap, red, low-cut party dress showed up for church on Sunday morning in a small town where everyone knew each other. The women began to whisper as soon as they saw her. Needless to say, the welcome mat was not rolled out. They did not know that the Sister Barber, the church's outreach minister, had witnessed to her the night before.

Sister Barber, had been walking through the park on her way home when she heard someone sobbing. Her eyes surveyed the area and found Candy. Sister Barber could see that Candy was a woman with a questionable reputation, but her compassion would not let her ignore Candy's pain. Sister Barber discovered that Candy had reached rock bottom. Sister Barber sat with Candy and told her about Jesus. She told Candy that she needed someone to be her guide. Then Sister Barber told Candy, *"I don't know a better guide than Jesus. Here is the address to my church. Stop by tomorrow for service and let me introduce you to him."*

Candy showed up early for church. She knew people would probably judge her, but she was determined not to let the unpleasant stares turn her around. She knew that she needed a guide, and she had decided that the guide would be Jesus.

APPLICATION

Sin is a small word with a big job. Sin is the biggest problem that human beings have ever encountered. All human beings, sinners and saved alike, have a propensity to sin. The apostle Paul said, *"I would do good, but evil is always present."* Sin is all around us. *"If you say you have no sin you are a liar and the truth is not in you."* Sin is like a maze, like a labyrinth. You can't find your way out; you need a guide to help you. Jesus Christ is the only capable guide.

It is only through Jesus Christ, the Lamb of God, who takes away the sins of the world we are saved. Jesus said, *"I am the way, the truth and the life, no man comes to the father but by me."* (John 14:6). If you confess with your mouth that Jesus Christ is Lord and believe in your heart that God raised him from the dead, you shall be saved (Romans 10:9-10). Only Jesus can save you. Only Jesus can redeem you. Only Jesus can justify you. Only Jesus can deliver you. Jesus is a worthy guide, a worthy savior, and a worthy God.

There comes a time in each life when life feels like an overwhelming flood, and suddenly you realize that you need a change. Accept the need of change. Find a church where you can connect with your guide named Jesus. Then consult with the pastor about a human guide. Establish regular meetings with your mentor/guide and begin to shape your new and exciting life in Jesus Christ.

PRAYER

Most Heavenly and all wise God, I want you to come into my life. I confess that I have been going down the wrong road, a road that has led to confusion, pain, and disaster. Change my direction, and guide me with your eye. Love me, save me, and keep me. Thank you for your amazing grace. Amen.

DAY 3

Salvation Comes from God through Christ

You Got the Right One, Baby...

"When the men were come unto him, they said,
John Baptist hath sent us unto thee, saying,
Art thou he that should come? or look we for another?
And in that same hour he cured many of their infirmities
and plagues, and of evil spirits; and unto many
that were blind he gave sight.
Then Jesus answering said unto them,
Go your way, and tell John what things ye have seen
and heard; how that the blind see,
the lame walk, the lepers are cleansed,
the deaf hear, the dead are raised,
to the poor the gospel is preached."

LUKE 7:20-22

Jesus' reputation had spread throughout all Judea because of the mighty works that he had done. John heard about the things that Jesus had done, so he sent men to ask Jesus if he was the Messiah they were waiting for. Jesus answered John's question by pointing to the works that he had done. In essence, Jesus' acts were saying, "You got the right one, baby."

Samantha spent a great deal of time rejecting her family and their religious tradition. She went full circle from Christianity to Buddhism, from Buddhism to Islam, from Islam to a variety of small cults and back to Christianity again. Shortly after returning to Christianity she began to question the authenticity of her faith. She met a friend who helped her to understand the dynamic between faith and doubt. Samantha's friend pointed her to the book of Luke to show her that even John the Baptist had doubts, but Jesus assured him that he was right. Whatever you need, Jesus has it. When you have Jesus, "You got the right one, baby."

APPLICATION

When trouble comes, we seem to fold up our faith and put it away in a closet. Our faith becomes stagnant, and doubt overtakes us like floodwaters overtake a drowning person. When doubt enters the picture there is only one thing we can do; we must do what John did, and go to Jesus.

Jesus is the right one. Jesus is the only one who can offer salvation. Read the following Scriptures, Acts 4:12;16:31, 2 Timothy 1:9

PRAYER

Lord Jesus, I know that you are the only one who has the power to offer salvation. I know that salvation comes only through the blood that you shed on the cross of Calvary. Thank you for leading me to the truth. I praise and adore your name for your goodness to me, for your love for me and for your amazing grace. Amen.

DAY 4

Salvation is for All

YOU CAN'T WIN WITH A LIFE OF SIN...

"Wherefore I say unto thee, her sins, which are many, are forgiven; for she loved much: but to whom little is forgiven, the same loveth little. And he said unto her, Thy sins are forgiven."

LUKE 7:47, 48

There was a small country where the people had been exploited and abused by those who were more privileged. A ruler emerged from among the people—one who was able to take charge and remove those who had exploited them. Eventually the leader began to assess the problems. One group that he wanted to redeem was a group of women who were forced into prostitution to survive. The leader offered them a new life. He gave them the opportunity to change their names, move to another part of the country, and enroll in a training program to gain some marketable skills. A good 98% of the prostitutes accepted the offer. This leader was able to see beyond the surface to the potential that the women possessed. Jesus did the same thing with the sinner who anointed him with oil.

The woman came giving instead of asking; she must have known something about Jesus. She must have been compelled to see Jesus, because she walked onto Simon's property and went directly to Jesus. She understood something about his greatness, because she would not face him. She knelt down and began to cry. Her tears provided the water needed to wash Jesus' feet. Her hair became a towel used to dry his feet. Her lips were used to kiss his feet. Then she anointed Jesus with oil from her alabaster box.

Who was this sinner woman? The only thing we know about her is that she was a sinner. Another book calls her a prostitute--a woman of the street. We think of a woman who spends a lot of time with many different men. Words like immoral or promiscuous come to mind. When we interact with people, we generally stop with what we see on the outside but Jesus looks on the inside.

While others passed judgement based on what they saw on the outside of this woman, Jesus knew the potential that lay beneath the surface. Jesus knew that life had taken her down some roads that created a bad reputation, a negative self-image, and an undesirable presence. He knew that her sins were many, and that she would be grateful for salvation.

APPLICATION

Jesus told the story to let Simon know that he knew about the woman and her lifestyle; and he knew Simon and what his attitude would be about forgiveness, but there was hope for the sinner woman.

Confess your sin. Proclaim your belief that Jesus Christ died for your sins, rose from the dead, ascended into heaven and one day will return for you. Change your lifestyle and begin to live for Jesus Christ.

PRAYER

Dear Lord, I am asking you to forgive my sins and to receive me into your kingdom. I believe that your Son, Jesus Christ, came into the world to save me, and I accept the free gift of salvation. I ask these things in the name of Jesus and for his sake. Amen.

DAY 5

Salvation Forever

A Drink that Satisfies…

*"Jesus answered and said unto her,
If thou knewest the gift of God,
and who it is that saith to thee,
Give me to drink; thou wouldest have asked of him,
and he would have given thee living water."*

JOHN 4:10

The woman at the well left her home to fetch a pail of water during the hottest part of the day, expecting to avoid contact with other human beings. However, she was surprised to find a Jewish man standing by the well. When the woman first met the man, she thought he was just an ordinary man, but she soon found

out that he was extraordinary. Jesus offered her living water; he offered a drink that satisfies. If the woman would drink the living water, she would never thirst again. "What kind of man is this? She thought, "This must be the Lord?"

APPLICATION

Have you ever been really, really thirsty? You try ice tea, pop, and juice but none of those seem to quench your thirst. On a very hot day, no matter what you try, nothing will quench your thirst like a tall glass of ice-cold water. You need a drink that satisfies. That is what the woman at the well needed.

Eventually she received the living water Jesus offered her. "Sir," the woman said, "I can see that you are a prophet." Now she saw Jesus for who he really is. She told Jesus about the prophecy of the Messiah who was to come, and Jesus did something unusual. He told the woman, "I that speak unto thee am he" (John 4:26). Jesus had set her up for the plan of salvation. After she received salvation, she when back into town saying, "Come, see a man who told me everything I ever did. Could this be the Christ?"

Witnessing is the natural consequence of conversion. Seek out someone this week and witness to them about something for which the Living Word of God has quenched your thirst. Tell them about the joy that you experienced by accepting the drink that Jesus had to offer offers.

PRAYER

Most Heavenly and all wise God, thank you for giving me a drink that satisfies. The new drink means that I can stop looking for satisfaction in all the wrong places. As he said, a drink from his fountain means that I will never thirst again. For this I praise you; I adore you; I magnify the matchless name of Jesus. Amen.

UNDERSTANDING THE CROSS

APRIL
WEEK FIVE: WOMEN OF GOD IN THE BIBLE

DAY 1
Tell o' Pharaoh

PHARAOH'S DAUGHTER AND QUEEN MOTHER MOORE…

"And the daughter of Pharaoh came down to wash herself at the river; and her maidens walked along by the river's side; and when she saw the ark among the flags, she sent her maid to fetch it. And when she had opened it, she saw the child: and, behold, the babe wept. And she had compassion on him."

EXODUS 2:5,6

The landscape in her hometown was ugly when Queen Mother Moore was born Audley Eloise Moore in 1898. She grew up hearing the stories of how African-American men had been lynched. Her grandfather had been lynched before his wife's eyes, and the women of his household had been raped. By the time she was 12 years old, she had witnessed much brutality against black people. By the time she was 15 years old, both her mother and father had died, and she was forced to leave school in order to support herself by doing hair.

However, it wasn't long before the struggle against oppression had become her life. She fought to change laws that would affect African-American children. She fought for the education of Black students in Brooklyn and New York. She organized a soup kitchen in Harlem for African students after two died of malnutrition, even though they had earned advanced degrees in the United States.

By the time that she was 74 years old, others had changed Audley's name to "Queen Mother Moore." Around the same time, she said, "Yes, I have done my best to measure up to qualify as a woman in the Black Movement. I have done my best." She died on May 2, 1997, at the age of 98.

In these stories we see two African women, separated by at least 3,000 years, living within vastly different cultures. One is a woman from a privileged Egyptian background, while the other is from a background of poverty and abuse. Both look out on a landscape in which an upcoming generation of people was under the threat of genocide. Both were surrounded by danger. In both cases, their very own lives could have been at risk.

Yet we see these two powerful Black women take a public stand. These two women are not unlike hundreds and thousands of African-American women who leave their homes every day and walk into environments where they must struggle on behalf of the oppressed. Today many of us are lawyers, judges, politicians, and managers in corporations that do business in the Black community. Many of us sit on boards that make decisions concerning the well-being of Black children. Many of us sit on juries and do the research used to design legislation that would make a difference for the upcoming generation.

APPLICATION

What does it take to stand up for righteousness, even when it means possibly losing our jobs? The first place to begin is with the fear of the Lord. If one fears the Lord, more than fearing human beings, one can act out of an energy that comes from outside oneself.

This week, as you put together your daily calendar, use a red pen to place a star beside those projects where you are challenged to stand up for righteousness. Think about the great host of witnesses (Hebrews 12:1-3) who are cheering you on. Think of witnesses such as Queen Mother Moore and pharaoh's daughter. Pray and walk out of your door in the power of God!

PRAYER

Lord, I have heard it said so many times that to whom much is given, much is expected. I have so much that my foremothers and forefathers didn't have. Yet sometimes it seems that the risks involved in standing up for the next generation are too much of a risk to take. Please give me, this day, the strength I need to do you proud and to make all of the strong black women that went before me proud. Thank you, Lord. Amen.

DAY 2

Backbones of a Race

Moses' Mother and Mother Bolton...

"And there went a man of the house of Levi, and took to wife a daughter of Levi. And the woman conceived, and bare a son: and when she saw him that he was a goodly child, she hid him three months. And when she could no longer hide him, she took for him an ark of bulrushes… and she laid it in the flags by the river's brink."

EXODUS 2:1-3

Linda could feel the grasp of her mother's hand as she sat across the desk from her teacher. It was a parent-teacher conference, and it was very formal. The teacher's words came like a death

knell, "It is perfectly clear that Linda is simply not college material," the teacher said in a cold, impersonal tone.

Linda could feel her mother's hand tighten its grip. Continuing with the cold tone, the teacher explained that the best tract for Linda would be home economics, a curriculum that would prepare her to be a good wife and mother. Linda felt her mother's hand tighten again. Then she felt herself being yanked as her mother stood up. "Thank you," her mother said, "but you will not have to concern yourself with my daughter's future. She will not be returning to this school next year."

Within a few months, Linda was on a Greyhound bus, heading for Kent School for Girls in the Berkshires of Connecticut. Today, Dr. Linda Bolton is an assistant professor of literature at the University of Iowa and a writer in the field of ethical philosophy.

"My mother truly believed in and taught me about the singular and collective power of women," she said. A graduate of the Art Institute of Chicago and the Illinois Institute of Technology, Mother Bolton was also a professor of art at Hampton University.

While Mother Bolton and Moses' mother are widely separated by time and culture, they share in common at least one thing—the challenge of being a mother in circumstances that threatened their child's existence. Today, most African-Americans can recount the stories of how our mothers came to our rescue when we were in danger. However, each of these stories is really a part of a larger story of the survival of an entire people. Great grandmother Jochebed (Moses' mother) is just one of the strong Black women who have formed the backbone of our race.

APPLICATION

Today, African-American women are still raising their children in adverse circumstances. The rate of black infant deaths is currently as high as it is in many developing countries Over three million African-American families with children are headed by women. The census shows that 9.1 million (at least 25 percent) of African-American families are in poverty.

Are you a mother, grandmother, great grandmother, adoptive mother, foster mother, or godmother? Where do you get the spiritual strength that it takes to meet this challenge in today's society?

Reflect on Psalm 23. What images of God come forth in that psalm? What do those traits of God have to do with the "mothering" gifts of God? How do they reflect on how God nurtures us within adverse circumstances? Are any of these traits reflected in Moses' mother and Loraine Williams Bolton? How can you cultivate these traits in your relationship with the children in your life? Make a list today, and pray over that list as God's mothering traits develop within you.

PRAYER

Oh, God. Help me to appreciate my role as mother in the lives of the children that you have placed within my life. Help me not to back down from the challenge of showing them your Spirit as they struggle with some of the most difficult challenges of their lives. Help me to delight in them. Help me to lead them in the paths of righteousness and to find ways to restore their souls. Amen.

DAY 3
Music in the Midst of a Storm

Miriam and Bernice…

"And Miriam the prophetess, the sister of Aaron, took a timbrel in her hand; and all the women went out after her with timbrels and with dances. And Miriam answered them, Sing ye to the Lord, for he hath triumphed gloriously; the horse and his rider hath he thrown into the sea."

EXODUS 15:20,21

Miriam, as the older sister of Moses, had a very vital role in bringing about his survival and thereby the survival of an entire community. However, her role was more than that. In some respects, she appears to have had much in common with Bernice Johnson Reagon who recalls a story of when she was at Albany

State College. It was a time when the Civil Rights struggle was escalating. Police had arrested some of her friends for trying to purchase bus tickets from the white window at the Trailways bus station. She and some of her other friends decided to march from campus in sympathy with them. But they only had a group of six or seven people.

Knowing that wasn't enough, she and her friends went around to classrooms to ask students to join them in the march. Still, only about ten people decided to leave campus. She faced forward and didn't look back. Then her friend, Annette, told her to look back quickly. "I looked and as far as I could see, all the way back to campus, there were people following. I tell you I never knew where they came from. I never heard them coming," she said.

APPLICATION

Today Bernice Johnson Reagon is the Distinguished Professor of History at American University, Curator Emeritus of the Smithsonian Institution, National Museum of American History, and founder of the a cappella ensemble, Sweet Honey in the Rock.

Bernice Johnson Reagon and Moses' sister are part of long tradition of African women. They share in common the gift of bringing music into difficult situations—music that healed, uplifted and had a prophetic voice. Miriam is described in Scripture as a prophet. We see her, down by the riverside, with her tambourine, belting out hymns of praise. She leads the people in song and dance. Then we see Bernice Johnson, thousands of years later, in the same role within yet another oppressed community—singing songs of hope, and songs of freedom, songs of protest, and songs of warning to the oppressors. Both Miriam and Bernice sang about God and helped to keep God at the center of the community during the times in which they lived. We need to praise God for the gift of preaching and song that God has brought into our lives through our women!

Reflect on Miriam's song today. Try to identify at least one gospel song that has similar themes. Play it today before you leave your house. Then, on your way to work, purchase a special card and send it to a female preacher or singer, telling her what a difference she has made in your life. Then pray and praise God for her.

PRAYER

Thank you, God, for music! Thank you for the art of Black preaching! Thank you for the powerful role that our songs have meant in our lives. Thank you for the creative way in which you helped us to survive and to be made closer to you. Thank you for the Miriams and Bernices that have enriched our lives! Amen.

DAY 4
Leave No Child Behind!

Shiphrah, Puah, and Miriam Wright Edelman...

"And the king of Egypt spake to the Hebrew midwives, of which the name of the one was Shiphrah, and the name of the other Puah: And he said, When ye do the office of a midwife to the Hebrew women, and see them upon the stools; if it be a son, then ye shall kill him: but if it be a daughter, then she shall live. But the midwives feared God, and did not as the king of Egypt commanded them, but saved the men children alive."

EXODUS 1:15-17

The mission of the Children's Defense Fund is to leave no child behind and to ensure that every child has a healthy, fair, safe, and moral start in life with the support of caring communities. Founded by Marian Wright Edelman, the CDF has become a strong national voice for children.

Edelman graduated from Yale University Law School during the turbulent 1960s. She was the first African-American woman admitted to the Mississippi Bar Association. She directed the NAACP Legal Defense and Educational Office and then served as the lawyer for Dr. Martin Luther King, Jr.'s, Poor People's March. She went on to found the Washington Research Project, which would later become the Children's Defense Fund.

In the article, "Standing up For the World's Children: Leave No Child Behind," Edelman says, "The great events of this world are not battles and elections and earthquakes and thunderbolts. The great events are babies, for each child comes with the message that God is not yet discouraged with humanity."

Edelman has quite a bit in common with Shiphrah and Puah. They all looked beyond the immediate moment. They decided to obey God and not be frightened of what others might say or do. When genocide was ordered, Shiphrah and Puah used their training to work against it. They had a choice. They could have thought only of themselves. They could have compromised. They could have found some way to get ahead by doing what pharaoh wanted. Instead, they decided to take the risk, knowing that in doing so, they were protected by God.

www.urbanspirit.biz

APPLICATION

Perhaps it is the stories of African women in the Bible like Shiphrah and Puah that inspired people like Marian Wright Edelman. We need to thank God for women who are on the front lines of the social struggles—the nurses, teachers, social workers, foster care parents, daycare workers, and crossing guards—and use use their special training to rescue the next generation.

In your prayer this morning, ask God to show you at least three ways that you can use your gifts to help an African-American child today. Write down the child's name and post it somewhere so that you will see it often. As ideas come, write them down and plan on acting on at least one of them during the next week.

PRAYER

Oh God, help us to remember each minute today the children who need help—your children. Show me what you would have me do for a child this week. Help me, like the midwives and Miriam Wright Edelman, to use my gifts to save the next generation. Amen.

DAY 5

Reaching into the Prisons

THE HEBREW MIDWIVES AND JANIE PORTER BARRETT...

"God dealt well with the midwives: and the people multiplied, and waxed very mighty. And it came to pass, because the midwives feared God, that he made them houses. And Pharaoh charged all his people, saying, Every son that is born ye shall cast into the river, and every daughter ye shall save alive."

EXODUS 1:20-22

Prison is no place for a young teenager. However, as early as the turn of the twentieth century, Janie Porter Barrett discovered hundreds of Black girls in adult prisons.

Janie was the daughter of parents who had been in slavery. After emancipation, they saw to it that she got an education, and she attended Hampton Institute (now Hampton University). She became a teacher but decided to remain within the sharecropping system of the rural South and taught sharecropper's children.

She established a daycare center in her home. When its growth reached a certain point, she organized it into the Locust Street Social Settlement. When she learned about the young women who were imprisoned, she opened the Virginia Industrial School for Colored Girls. She got support from other African-American women, along with funding from foundations. The program soon became an official part of the Virginia Department of Social Services. She retired as superintendent of the school in 1940 and died on August 27, 1948.

Janie has something in common with the Hebrew midwives, Shiphrah and Puah. Like them, she was among a community of African women and came upon a troubling situation. She decided to join forces with other women and, with God's help, to solve the problem. Like the midwives, she didn't waste her time competing for power with her sisters in ministry. Instead, she focused on a problem and created a sense of collegiality among her sisters.

APPLICATION

We need to thank God for all of the strong Black women who, throughout the ages, have pulled together and made changes in the world. They have worked together in the African-American church, in the sororities, in the professional associations, in the block clubs, and in the extended families, in the Parent Teacher Associations, and in the Local School Councils. Praise God for the spiritual energy to work together for our common good!

Recall some of the organizations in your church or community where African-American women work together on projects that result in the improvement of the church and in outreach to troubled youth. Add them to your prayer list. Mention their work before God today. Ask God to help you support their efforts.

PRAYER

Oh, God, help me to work with my sisters in ministry on projects that will result in the salvation and survival of young people throughout our community. Give me your Spirit of cooperation. Cast out any evil spirits of jealousy and competition. Help us to keep the tradition of self-help and sisterhood alive in our communities. Thank you, O God, for allowing me to be a part of your kingdom work. Amen and Amen!

BEING A WOMAN IS SPECIAL

MAY
WEEK ONE: MOTHERING

DAY 1

Mothering, What a Privilege!

FOCUS ON GOD…

*"But seek ye first the kingdom of God,
and his righteousness;
and all these things shall be added unto you."*
MATTHEW 6:33

My dream as a young girl playing with dolls was to someday become a mother. Even as I grew beyond those early years, I was occupied by thoughts of earnestly and sincerely giving of myself to nurture a tender seedling placed in my care by God.

Our first child, a son, came without a prayer and seemingly without much effort on our part; just

sheer biology. However, it would be 10 years before God intervened and blessed us with a second child for whom I had deeply longed. Why did the ugly head of infertility rear itself, thwarting our plans? I thought that because our first child's conception seemed so easy, the same would happen when we decided to have our second child.

I had many sad days when hope was waning and my dream of another child seemed impossible. I shared my sadness with my pastor and friends to help shoulder the pain. I sometimes felt ashamed as I spoke with the Lord in prayer, for after all I did have one child. But my desire for another grew stronger. One day in the quietness of my home, the Spirit of the Lord whispered to my spirit, "Just leave this to me. Give away the baby things and put your trust in me."

Like Hannah, I wept bitterly and cried out to God. Month after month and year after year, the message came to me by the Spirit, "Seek first the kingdom." During those times, I realized that my dreams and desires were secondary to my relationship with Christ. I also realized that I had allowed things other than God to dominate my thoughts and actions and to become the center of my life. Once I began to really "know the Savior," it no longer mattered what my dreams were; I just wanted his will for my life.

APPLICATION

God is a jealous God. He demands that we place him in the center of our marriages, our homes, and our relationships.

We can know God's will for us if we seek him first, study his Word, and build a relationship with him.

Whether it's infertility or some other problem that dominates your thoughts and energy, redirect your focus toward the Lord and his Word. Surround yourself with praying Christians who will hold you up in prayer if your faith falters or you lose hope. Allow God to minister to you as you wait for his divine intervention in your life.

Spend an hour in extra quiet time with God today or determine what day soon you can do that, and schedule that hour on your calendar.

PRAYER

Dear Lord, I love you and want to please you. I worship and adore you. I pray this day that you will bless me as you did your servant, Hannah. I pray your will be done in my life as I yield myself to you. I pray for other people who are carrying the burden of unfulfilled hopes and dreams. Draw them nearer to you and bless them. Amen.

DAY 2

Threats to Motherhood

GIVE THE FUTURE TO GOD...

"Thou shalt not be afraid for the terror by night; nor for the arrow that flieth by day; Nor for the pestilence that walketh in darkness; nor for the destruction that wasteth at noonday."

PSALM 91:5,6

One Sunday, my pastor gave a stirring sermon on the subject of threats and how to cope with them. He told us that there were threats to our health, our jobs, our marriages, our relationships—threats that affect our lives on a daily basis. As I thought about what he said, the Holy Spirit began to bring to mind the threats that mothers face as we raise our children in the ways of our Lord and Savior. How could I as a Christian mother hold up a standard of righteousness for my children when they were bombarded with the temptation of drugs and alcohol, and were threatened by sexual exploitation, violence, and crime? Satan is our enemy, and he wants to corrupt our children and turn them from the faith of their fathers and mothers. I worried that these threats would devour my children and make me an ineffective mother.

I committed myself to pray for my children each day as they went to school, attended parties, drove the family car, met new friends, and went on their first dates. "Lord," I prayed, "bring other teens into their lives who will have a positive impact on them. Let your spirit draw them to you." I prayed that God would prepare mates for them when the time was right for marriage. I asked our Father to build a hedge of protection around them during the impressionable years. I could not take them out of our society to keep them from harm, but I could put a "prayer covering" over them on a daily basis.

APPLICATION

Do you want Satan to snatch away your child's destiny? Are you aware of the threats to your child's welfare that lurk all around? Take the offensive, stand strongly in the gap, and intercede for your child's very life and soul. Each day set a time aside, close out the world, and offer your child to God. In the name of Jesus, ask for boldness and strength to stand against the enemy.

List things that you want for your child. Then lift that list up to God in prayer.

PRAYER

God, grant me the spirit of boldness to stand against the threats of the enemy and to declare righteousness. I have no power within myself to protect my children, so as I raise them, I yield myself to you and ask for your wisdom and guidance. Amen.

DAY 3
Thank God Mothering Isn't just for Mothers!

USE YOUR GIFT...

*"And the King shall answer and say unto them,
Verily I say unto you,
Inasmuch as ye have done it unto one of the least
of these my brethren, ye have done it unto me."*

MATTHEW 25:40

A woman who was going through the process of adopting a 15-year-old girl with many behavioral challenges sent me a poem. It was entitled, "Thank God Mothering is Not Just for Mothers." In the poem she thanked me, as her adoption social worker, as well as all of the people who had played a role in the life of her 15-year-

old girl. Her poem stated, "People like you mother the children who are between families." The poem went on to express gratitude to all five of the foster families who gave temporary nurture and care to her child, to the birth parents for giving her child life, to the residential staff who provided for her child's needs, and to the mentor who came occasionally to just hang out with her troubled teen.

APPLICATION

How can we help? Who stands in the gap for these children? Who is committed to lifting them up in prayer as they face an uncertain future? Even if being a full-time adoptive or foster mother is out of the question for you, consider the role of mentor. Do you know a young mother who would enjoy having a mature Christian woman share a cup of coffee with her? God has endowed women with the unique ability to nurture children. For those who have not borne children, there are so many ways to express that God-given gift. You do not need to be a mother to do mothering. A mother is one who can positively influence people for the glory of God. Look for ways to help others as you go about your daily routine. Let the Spirit of the Lord direct and guide you to the person whose needs you can meet.

Take a child on a special outing. Learn the joy of being part of the village that raises a child.

PRAYER

Dear Lord, I long to care for and bring comfort to others. Direct my path. Help me to prefer others above myself in love. There are so many people who need you, Lord. Please let your light shine through me so that they can be drawn to your saving grace. Amen.

DAY 4

Super Mother

ENJOY...

"I can do all things through Christ which strengtheneth me."

PHILIPPIANS 4:13

She is able to stop a speeding bottle and leap over 20 toy trains in a single bound. She cooks, she sews, and she balances many different tasks in the blink of an eye. She shops with two toddlers and is able to safely move from one aisle to another while she juggles one child on her hip and drives the other in the cart with the groceries. She is super woman! She works part-time in her home business while the children are taking their naps on the mat by her knees. When she puts her head down at night, she prays to the Lord for his strength to get up the next day and begin all over.

Does this sound anything like you or any mother that you know? Well, this is a picture of many women who struggle to balance the responsibilities of work and children. Whether single or married, the pressures in our fast-paced society are astounding.

When I was a young mother, my husband traveled all over the country, leaving me to take care of children, pay bills, do all the household chores (including shoveling snow and mowing the lawn). Did I say that I worked full-time? I remember falling on my knees one evening, exhausted, with no strength left to drag myself to bed. I turned on the radio and heard the song, "Yes, Jesus Loves Me." The song filled me with joy and the love of Christ enraptured me. I was reassured that Jesus was offering me his strength and peace. I began to sing that little song on a daily basis, letting the words minister to me. My vigor and energy were renewed as I read his Word and shared my thoughts with him in silent prayer and meditation.

APPLICATION

When life's daily challenges threaten to overwhelm you and you seem to be losing out on the blessings and joys of motherhood, plan a quiet time with the Savior. Ask for his strength and power to perform your daily tasks. Focus on a favorite verse or sing a well-loved song to God. This will bring refreshment and a sense of peace to your spirit.

Don't spend all of today working. Take your child out to a special place. Relax and enjoy the spontaneous moment. Let God bless your time together.

PRAYER

Slow me down, Lord, so that I may hear from you and order my day according to your will and desire. Let me love my children as much as you love me, your child. Help me to realize that I do not have to be a super mother but rather a yielded mother to Christ. Oh, Lord, your strength is my joy. Amen.

DAY 5
Mothering the Mother

BLESS THE MOTHERS...

"For Moses said, Honour thy father and thy mother; and, Whoso curseth father or mother, let him die the death."

MARK 7:10

My dear little gray-haired mother worked two jobs to keep her seven children in proper clothes and food while living in public housing project. A young widow, she successfully raised all of us to adulthood. We each have a college degree or a technical skill that enables us to achieve a satisfactory quality of life. Not once did she have to bail us out of jail, deal with a drug abusing child, or, worse than that, bury one

of us prematurely as a victim of gang violence or reckless behavior. After obtaining her GED at the ripe old age of 50, she went from welfare to workfare. She never let complacency, apathy, or excuses overtake her or dictate her life. She always walked with her head high, her shoulders tall, and a quick, steady pace. What was it about her that kept her focused on her children and their future, instead of complaining, blaming, and feeling ashamed? It would have been easy to crumble under the weight of the routine pressures of motherhood.

APPLICATION

As I examined my dear mother's qualities, it became apparent to me that she was not alone, Jesus was always with her. When I was growing up, my mother used to sing simply and sweetly, "Jesus Is My Friend." And he was. Jesus was with her: as a friend, a husband, and a comforter during her long, lonely days as a single mother. He was there to strengthen and provide for her children through her church, her neighbors, and relatives who took some of us into their homes when times were particularly difficult.

Now, as she faces her golden years with blurred vision, dulled hearing, and a shortened stride, she still sings her song. I now know what she means when she sings, "Jesus is my friend."

Take your mother or a mentor out to lunch. You will bless them, and God will bless you by their wisdom.

PRAYER

Dear Lord, remind us of the importance of giving back to our parents when they are in their later years. Give us the patience and wisdom to know how to minister to them in a loving way. Lord, whether they have to be in a nursing home or in our home, give them comfort, peace, and provision. Amen.

BEING A WOMAN IS SPECIAL

MAY
WEEK TWO: CHILDREN

DAY 1
God's Great Miracle

MY SWEET BABY...

"Lo, children are an heritage of the Lord: and the fruit of the womb is his reward."

PSALM 127:3

Devetta had done enough reading and research on childbirth to write her own dissertation on the topic! She and her husband had tried for seven years to conceive. Finally, their prayer petitions had been answered. Now it was only a matter of days before their bundle of joy would arrive. But a year ago she had not been so full of joy.

Devetta dialed her friend Karen, a veteran mom and newfound spiritual adviser. "Hey girl, come join me for a big tuna salad and a V-8."

Karen, picking up on her friend's giddiness, recalled what a difference a year had made and how it was not that long ago that she thought she would never hear her friend sound joyful again. "God is certainly good all the time," Karen quipped.

"And all the time, God is good," Devetta quickly shot back.

"You know, birth is truly the most miraculous display of God's omnipotence. How could anyone ever have any doubt as to his power, mercy and goodness?" said Karen. Even during the years of trying, trying, trying, Devetta knew it was all in God's hands.

"Oh, oh, girl! My water just broke. Oh, sweet Jesus. My miracle is about to take place. Let me call Ray; we will definitely have to put that salad on hold."

APPLICATION

The abundant joy felt by an expectant mother is something that is never articulated exactly the same way by any two mothers. Yet a common sentiment in the Christian mother's voice is the voice of reassurance that she is about to deliver God's blessing; a child born not only unto her, but also unto the Lord.

Today, if you are counting the days before the arrival of your bundle of joy—whether this is your first or one of several—relish and frolic in this time. Enjoy the goodness and kindness of others. Forget career pressures and know that your time with God, self, and this precious bundle is most important.

Breathe deeply, release all anxieties, and embrace this moment. Soon, your world will change completely, but God will be with you, every step of the way. You are a crowned queen who has been blessed with the most powerful position on earth: Mother.

PRAYER

Precious Savior, I humbly thank you for this blessing. For the rest of my days, I will honor you by loving this child unconditionally. Lord, thank you for entrusting this child to me. I will love and protect my child and raise him or her to be a righteous child of God. Hear my prayer in the name of your precious Son, Amen.

DAY 2

A Child's Death

Lord, Help Me To Hold Out...

*"The sting of death is sin;
and the strength of sin is the law.
But thanks be to God, which giveth us the victory
through our Lord Jesus Christ."*

1 CORINTHIANS 15:56, 57

Renee and Donna were talking about two friends who had both lost young children. Donna said, "Girl, they would have to bury me, too, if something ever happened to my child. There's just no way I could go on."

Renee was speechless for a moment. The women who had lost their children had been

hardworking and God-fearing. They were as kind and righteous as they come, yet look what had happened to them. But they still praised God's holy and righteous name every day without hesitation. "Girl, they must have incredible strength. I mean, I know he doesn't give us more than we can bear, but if that's not more than one can bear, tell me what is?"

"Well, these mothers knew, as did their children, that Christ is always by our side, even in the storm. That does not mean that their pain is not real, but they know that Christ wept for Lazarus, and they know they can turn to their Father in heaven for comfort. The Scripture tells us, "Blessed are they that mourn: for they shall be comforted" (Matthew 5:4).

APPLICATION

At the loss of a loved one, there are few words that comfort. The pain, especially when one loses a child, is incomprehensible. It goes as deep as the sharpest blade; it feels as if one is suffocating. Swallowed up in pain, we may not want to hear words of comfort. Yet, in the midst of it all, we can count on the little voice that reminds us through the tears that Christ is always with us. Yes, through the pain, shock, denial, he is there. The Bible tells us, "I will turn their mourning into joy, and will comfort them, and make them rejoice from their sorrow" (Jeremiah 31:13).

If you are facing sorrow, take one day at a time. It's all right to heal at your own pace. Seek shelter in God's loving arms, which are strong enough to carry you. It is okay to shy away from family and friends who cannot help you at this time. Do not forsake your health during this time; rest and food are essential, as is the company of those who understand. Aim at the goal of being able to praise God's holy name.

PRAYER

Oh Lord, my heavenly Father, I cannot bear this heavy burden alone. I hand it to you, Father. Take it away, I beg of you, and replace it with your peace. You know how much I ache inside. Fill me with the Spirit of the Holy Ghost and carry me in your loving arms until I have the strength to stand. I ask this in the name of your son, Jesus Christ, Amen.

DAY 3
A Child's Illness
Lord, Make it Go Away!

*"Let your conversation be without covetousness;
and be content with such things as ye have:
for he hath said, I will never leave thee,
nor forsake thee."*

HEBREWS 13:5

"What's wrong Pam?" Denise asked. "You sound like you haven't gotten a bit of sleep all night."

"Is it that obvious?" Pam asked right back. "You're right though. I don't think I got a wink. At least it doesn't feel as if I did. Gary's asthma had us both up all night. Girl, sometimes all I can do is cry my eyes out thinking about my poor baby boy."

"Leave it at the altar girl," Denise retorted. "You know you have no business carrying this around. It's no good for you or Gary."

"That is real easy to say, Denise, but you have no idea what you're talking about. Your kids are all healthy!"

"Then let's just open the Good Book and find a Scripture that says the same thing," said Denise. "One of my favorites is in the Psalms: 'The Lord is thy keeper: the Lord is thy shade upon thy right hand. The sun shall not smite thee by day, nor the moon by night. The Lord shall preserve thee from all evil: he shall preserve thy soul. The Lord shall preserve thy going out and thy coming in from this time forth, and even for evermore' (Psalm 121:5-8)."

Pamela wrapped her arms around Denise. "Girl, I get it. I've been so lost in my own self I haven't heard these beautiful words in a long time. Thanks, lady."

APPLICATION

Sometimes we become so lost in the problem, we don't even realize the solution has been provided. But it's all here in his divine Word. No one intends to minimize what you might be going through with a sick child, especially if the illness is chronic or terminal. But God knows, my sister. Take it to the altar and throw it out there. Cast your burdens away with conviction, not carelessness. God is a loving and caring God and doctor of all doctors. He has the prescription to fix it, but you've got to take it to his pharmacy. In his time, he will provide the perfect remedy.

In order to care for a sick child, you must care for yourself. Are you eating properly? Getting enough rest and exercise? Yes, exercise! No excuses are allowed. You are not going to be of service to anyone, especially your child, if you are not maintaining your own health. Eat a healthy meal, walk a few blocks, and rest. Now pray. Whatever prayer comes to mind, just pray and leave it with the Lord. Don't claim it again from this point on. Leave your problem at the altar.

PRAYER

Lord, my problem is in your hands, my precious and faithful Savior. I present it to you, and I know you will do mighty things. Hear my prayer, Oh Lord, as I release my burden, in the name of your Son, Amen.

DAY 4
Wild Child

THE BROTHER'S LOST!

*"Correct thy son, and he shall give thee rest;
yea, he shall give delight unto thy soul.
Where there is no vision, the people perish:
but he that keepeth the law, happy is he."*

PROVERBS 29:17-18

Charlotte was exhausted. Quite frankly, she was exasperated. The stress of her job was heavy upon her shoulders as she dragged herself along the aisle in the meat department, trying to find a quick meal. I don't know why I still bother, Charlotte thought to herself. He has become so ungrateful. No matter what I bring home, he'll pitch a fit.

"Hey Lady," Brenda called Charlotte back from her daydream. "How've you been? Haven't seen you at church lately. Sister Carolyn's Bible study has become so crowded, I don't know if you're on the other side of the church or not."

Charlotte declared, "Hey girl. No, I'm afraid I've been a bit absent. If I don't get straight home from work to keep my eye on the boys, it's no telling what I'll find when I walk in the house. Bruce has become so full of himself as a teenager that sometimes I'm actually afraid of my own son. He's not my little boy anymore, that's for sure. He's skipping school and doing things he never would have done before."

Out in the parking lot, Brenda continued, "Girl, I can't say I know what you're going through," Brenda said, "but I do know that now is not the time to walk away from the church; you've got to stay with the Word. You may feel that God does not hear you, but it is at this time that your voice is the loudest. Stop and listen to him."

APPLICATION

Ecclesiastes 3:1-2 tells us that there is a time for everything. Know that God will not forsake you as you struggle to rein in an unruly child. Remain in the Word at this time when the pain is so personal. You gave birth to this child, and you have done all that is humanly possible to raise him or her up right. Drop to your knees, my sister, and know that this too shall pass.

Encourage your "demanding" child with positive words. If possible, find a positive role model or mentor from your church or the community who will get involved in his or her life. Oftentimes, children act out because they want attention or are stressed by peer pressure and are not mature enough to articulate how they feel. Finally, do not blame yourself—realize that this battle is not yours but the Lord's.

PRAYER

Heavenly Father, help me to remain strong for my child. Lord, I don't know what happened to make my child go down the wrong path, but I'm asking you to straighten the crooked places. Touch my child's heart and soul, and return my child to your will. I thank you Lord. In the name of Jesus. Amen.

DAY 5

Spiritual Growth

Yes Lord, That's My Baby!

"Train up a child in the way he should go, even when he is old he will not depart from it."

PROVERBS 22:6

"Wow, look how she has grown," Cynthia declared. "It seems as if only yesterday she was in your arms. Megan, you must be so proud of her."

Megan beamed as she sat and watched her little girl singing in the choir at the children's chapel. The fourth Sunday was always a full house, with proud parents and grandparents racing to get the front pews to see the performance of their little pride and joy.

"Yes, Lord, that's my baby! Go 'head sweetie, you can do it," Megan shouted, as little Melissa approached the microphone for her first solo. She had done such a fine job in the Christmas recital where the more-seasoned children normally dominate, that the choir director felt it was time to let the smaller ones shine for the Lord.

"How do you do it?" Cynthia asked. "I mean, you have Melissa in the choir, Devin is the junior Bible class leader, and Denise is on the junior usher board. Girl, tell me your secret. I can barely get J-J to read his Bible regularly, and the Sunday school teacher is always sending notes home about him playing around."

Megan declared, "It's no secret. I'm just doing what my Momma did for us. She taught us to love the Lord before we were weaned from the bottle! There was never any force, no bribing. Momma read us the Scripture along with our nursery rhymes. I can only pray that I'm training up my children in the same way by providing such an early Christian education. Girl, I'm sure J-J will do the same. Hey, let's let our children begin studying and worshiping together!"

APPLICATION

There is no greater joy than to watch a child absorb the teachings of the gospel. What a joyful noise it is to hear our own children sing out in his holy name, to see them engage in the Bible school teachings, and become active in the youth and young adult ministries. Jesus said, "Verily I say unto you, whosoever shall not receive the kingdom of God as a little child shall in no wise enter therein" (Luke 18:17).

Teach your babies by example. Let them see you in the Word, let them know you live the Word, and guide them to emulate all that you do to promote his kingdom. It is never too early—or too late for that matter—to teach our children how to love the Lord.

PRAYER

Heavenly Father, guide me as I instruct and teach my precious jewels all that is in your name, so they may teach others to do your holy and righteous will. In the name of your son, Jesus Christ, Amen.

BEING A WOMAN IS SPECIAL

MAY
WEEK THREE: HOMEMAKER

DAY 1
The Value of Homemaking

FINDING SUPPORT

"Strength and honour are her clothing; and she shall rejoice in time to come."

PROVERBS 31:25

Elizabeth called up her friend Deirdre. "Girl! What's up? We haven't talked in about two years. Time has gotten away from us."

Deirdre responded, "I know, but we can change that!" They both chuckled.

Their long-distance conversation lasted for over two hours. The majority of the conversation was about Elizabeth and her husband's encouragement to change careers.

Deirdre said, "Are you serious? You are going to do what—be a full-time homemaker? What made you decide to be a homemaker?"

Elizabeth excitedly explained to Deirdre that she and Eric had committed their decision to prayer. She realized that some people would question their decision, but they were eager for their family to grow as the Lord chose to bless them with children.

APPLICATION

The challenge today seems to come not from choosing a career outside the home, but from choosing to stay home. Some women either disagree with or don't understand the privilege of being a homemaker. Deciding to become a full-time homemaker is no different from deciding to become a doctor or a lawyer. When we choose homemaking as a career, the Lord faithfully meets our spiritual, physical, and emotional needs, even when we face challenges and insults. It was said of Jesus, "When he was reviled, reviled not again; when he suffered, he threatened not; but committed himself to him that judgeth righteously (1 Peter 2:23).

We, too, can handle challenges by keeping our focus on God and by turning to him for instruction on how to handle the specific situation. Proverbs encourages us to trust in the Lord with all our hearts, not to lean on our own understanding (3:5,6), and to commit our works to the Lord (16:3). Psalms tells us to delight ourselves in him (37:4-6).

1. Seek a mentoring relationship with an older Christian homemaker: "The aged women likewise...may teach the young women to be sober, to love their husbands, to love their children" (Titus 2: 3-4).

2. Memorize a Bible verse that speaks for you in your heart's desire to be a homemaker.

PRAYER

Thank you, Lord, for allowing me to consider the blessed vocation of homemaking. Help me to glorify you every day at home as I would at work. Amen.

DAY 2
Contentment As a Homemaker

*"And whatsoever ye do, do it heartily,
as to the Lord, and not unto men;
knowing that of the Lord ye shall receive the reward
of the inheritance: for ye serve the Lord Christ."*

COLOSSIANS 3:23-24

People were having a great debate about the least and the greatest. One person stated what he would require and listed how people would serve him if he were the greatest person on earth. Another person stood up and stated how he would handle the world if he were the greatest person on earth. He said he would share his riches with family and friends, and give to those less fortunate!

APPLICATION

If you had been present during this debate, what would you have said? Within you is there a desire for a position of dominance, significance, and wealth? Or are you content in whatever state you are in?

Let's ask the Lord to grant us these things: peace and contentment with our position; a kind, willing, and humble heart; and a desire to give and share with others. Our goal should be contentment in our daily walk as we do all that we can to glorify and honor the Lord. A change of perspective will allow truth to fill our hearts to overflowing and influence the lives of many. As we come to understand the power of obedience, we do all that we do "as unto the Lord."

Set yourself the goal of doing one special thing for someone each day in service to the Lord. Write it out on a seven-day chart.

Plan to do a craft activity with your children—or cook a fun family meal—and use the time as the setting to share, in a couple of sentences, what you are learning.

PRAYER

Thank you, Lord, for giving me an understanding of the value of achievement and success. Help me make decisions in the light of your truth and make the most of every opportunity. May you be glorified in all that I do and say. Amen.

DAY 3
THE WORTH OF THE HOMEMAKER

*"Who can find a virtuous woman?
For her price is far above rubies."*

PROVERBS 31:10

Traci and Nichole were having their usual discussion of relationships. They both felt that a relationship should have a purpose. They both thought that there was a good possibility that the young man she one was dating would be the one she would marry.

Traci said, "My mother and I discussed my relationship with Gregory. She thinks that he is a great guy and wanted to know what I thought about him."

Nichole responded, "Girl, you've got such a great relationship with your mom. My mother died when I was only 7. My dad never remarried, and I've never had anyone to have the mother and daughter talks with like you have. Things are great between me and my dad, but I miss having a mother."

Traci smiled at her friend before she responded, "You know, my mother really thinks a lot of you. She considers you to be like her own daughter. So, don't hesitate to call her sometime to talk. She would love that."

Tears came to Nichole's eyes as she smiled back at her friend, and said: "Okay. Just remember that I want to be in your wedding."

APPLICATION

Our desire, as godly women, should be to live in a way that is pleasing to God, laying aside manipulation and selfish motives, and seeking instruction from the Word. Living a surrendered life that pleases the Lord is a different life to that lived by the woman who lives for herself. Be the woman God created you to be.

If you are single person who wants to be a homemaker, be willing to discuss this honestly and openly with your husband-to-be.

If you are married but feel financially unable to be a homemaker, discuss the situation with your husband and develop a financial plan to enable your family to live on one income.

If you are a homemaker, make the most of this opportunity. Set goals, standards, and boundaries to benefit your family. Discuss your ideas with your husband, and don't procrastinate. Seek to build relationships with other homemakers to encourage each other.

—and enjoy your career choice.

PRAYER

Lord, the career choices are many. Please encourage each of us in our choice, and grant special joy and appreciation to those who choose homemaking as a career. Amen.

DAY 4
Creativity as a Homemaker

"Withhold not good from them to whom it is due, when it is in the power of thine hand to do it.
PROVERBS 3:27

Every Wednesday after the children's choir rehearsal, Janice and Brian took their four children to Jason's Deli for family fun. There was always a clown at the deli who painted the children's faces.

A visiting playmate, Bria, was planning to accompany the Evans family on a particular Wednesday. There was uncertainty as to how she would feel going to meet the clown and being surrounded by people she didn't know. Bria was a paraplegic. Her wheelchair was decorated

creatively, and she always wore cute clothes. Yet, Bria was sometimes shy in unfamiliar surroundings.

Brian and Janice decided not to change their weekly Wednesday fun night because Bria was to be with them. They expected Bria would have a great time, and she did. She wasn't embarrassed or shy. She enjoyed the clown and the face painting, and had a fun time with friends of Brian and Janice's family.

APPLICATION

Sometimes we shy away from uncomfortable situations. Saturated with fear, we run marathons to get out of such a situation. Despite challenges, our hearts' desire should be to love and serve people, help them to be successful, and encourage them to step out of their comfort zones.

"Beloved, let us love one another: for love is of God; and everyone that loveth is born of God and knoweth God. He that loveth not knoweth not God; for God is love" (I John 4:7-8).

Think of a family member, friend, or neighbor for whom you could do something that would make smile. Be creative. You could take flowers to an elderly person, bake cookies with a neighbor's child, take a plant to a friend, or deliver balloons to your spouse to say, "I love you."

PRAYER

Lord, as a homemaker we have time to spend making other people happy. Thank you for those blessed opportunities.

DAY 5
POWER OF COMMITMENT

"Every wise woman buildeth her house: but the foolish plucketh it down with her hands."

PROVERBS 14:1

The Sunday newspaper had an article that Alicia thought was strange. It discussed the values and roles of godly women, but there was no mention of women who chose to commit themselves to their families as full-time homemakers.

Alicia emailed the newspaper editor to ask why the role of homemaker had been omitted. The editor emailed Alicia back with an apology for the oversight. The following Sunday, the paper had a further article, this time on the role of homemaker. The title was, "There is Great Value in the Position of Homemaker." Alicia was

elated. The article encouraged the acceptance of women who choose to be homemakers and to focus on having an impact on the future of their husbands, children, family, and friends.

For the woman who accepts the call to be a homemaker, the guidance, encouragement, peace, and grace of the Lord is a must. When she lacks wisdom, she should ask God, who gives it generously (James 1:5). The peace of God (Philippians 4:7) will give her comfort when challenges come.

Sometimes friends or family members may challenge the decision to be a homemaker; they may not see the value in this decision, fearing the loss of educational, financial, or career opportunities. Everything necessary to be a successful homemaker is found in Jesus, and regular Bible study is a help in making godly decisions (2 Timothy 3:16-17).

APPLICATION

Don't allow other people to discourage you from your commitment to your family. Remember Colossians 3:17: "And whatsoever ye do in word or deed, do all in the name of the Lord Jesus, giving thanks to God and the Father by him."

Look at what your family presently needs, and then create a fun project to fulfill those needs. Your family will benefit from your commitment. "Her children arise up, and call her blessed; her husband also, and he praiseth her" (Proverbs 31:28).

PRAYER

Father, you have given the precious yet powerful and influential role of motherhood to women. Please give clarity of the call, freedom in the experience, and joy to all who accept the call of homemaker.

BEING A WOMAN IS SPECIAL

MAY
WEEK FOUR: ESTHER

DAY 1
Time out for Beauty

DISCOVER THE SPIRIT WITHIN...

"Favour is deceitful, and beauty is vain: but a woman that feareth the Lord, she shall be praised."

PROVERBS 31:30

Today we are bombarded with manufacturers' promotions and advertising promises to improve our physical appearance. Manufacturers have products that change the texture of our hair, lighten our skin, remove cellulite, enhance our breasts, whiten our teeth, smooth the wrinkles in our faces, improve the appearance of our hands, and so on.

Our hopes of improving our lives and our self-worth have distracted us from developing the inner spiritual woman. There comes a time when we need to rebuild what is on the inside. We need to rekindle our heritage by fasting, prayer, and meditation, and then resolve the challenges in our lives. We need to give thanks, and praise the Lord. We need to take time out to recognize the victory God has given us in particular areas of our lives and celebrate the beauty he is creating within us.

Let's take a look at Esther (in the book of Esther). She was invited to participate in a beauty pageant. Esther was put in a harem with the most beautiful women in the land. These women lived their entire lives using their charm to survive. They had the finest perfumes, jewelry, and clothes available, with expert clothing designers, and with dietitians and beauticians grooming them to perfection. Can you imagine the spiritual nature of these women? Imagine the jealousy, the vanity, the superficial attitudes, the self-indulgence, and the egotistical spirits floating through this harem of divas. You get the picture? Does this remind you of anything in our time—on television, in church, in school, or on the job?

APPLICATION

In the midst of all this negative energy, Esther stood out. Her inner beauty, strength, and dignity dominated the room. The king's chamberlain recognized the special qualities that radiated from Esther, qualities that went beyond Esther's physical attributes. When she appeared before the king, it was her wit, obedience, and teachable spirit that melted his heart and won her the crown of queen.

Look in the mirror. Focus on your physical reflection. Write down what you like about what you see. Write down what you don't like about what you see.

Go back and look in the mirror again. Focus on the inner woman. Try to see your spiritual reflection. Write down what you like about what you "see." Write down what you don't like about what you "see."

PRAYER

Lord, thank you for allowing me to take time out for beauty. Help me to recognize the beautiful woman within. Help me to build on my special uniqueness. Make me discontent with my superficial nature. Deepen my desire to develop the inner spiritual woman, to cultivate the virtuous woman who lives within me. Amen.

DAY 2

Keeping in Touch

KNOW YOUR HERITAGE...

"One generation shall praise thy works to another, and shall declare thy mighty acts."

PSALMS 145:4

It was a typical lunch day for the corporate clique. Nearby in the corporate cafeteria, an elderly African-American woman, who had worked there for years, was celebrating with her family and friends her 35th anniversary of work. The corporate clique watched the celebration from a nearby table. An undercurrent of cynicism began to emerge like a cloud of smoke. They mocked the elderly lady's guests with comments about unfashionable attire, dated hairstyles, and questionable table manners. Discreet laughter

was followed by one shameless, impolite comment after another.

"Sweet and graceful and melodious" would be a fair and respectful description of this elderly African-American woman. She was the aunt or grandmother we all are familiar with in the African-American community: she always had a smile, a Scripture, and a kind word. I had bumped into her on several occasions. In our conversations, I had learned that she had adopted several children and, although she was not able to finish school herself, had sent these children to college. She reminded me of my own self-sacrificing family. I was ashamed that the people at my table would despise this woman's sacrifice.

APPLICATION

When we move away from home, experience new things, become accustomed to a new way of living, eat at fine restaurants, and shop at prestigious stores, we can easily forget where we came from. Staying in touch with our heritage keeps us humble and grounded. In the Old Testament we read about how Esther had to be reminded of her heritage. As queen, she was exposed to a new way of life. She had access to the finest foods, and the comforts that come along with living in a royal palace.

One day her cousin Mordecai, a Jew living in exile, contacted her. Mordecai reminded Esther of her heritage by telling her that she was a Jew, and that no Jew would escape Haman's plot. Once she connected with her past, her fear and insecurity diminished. Esther became secure in the Lord, and an inner strength emanated from her.

Today, if you are out of fellowship with your past—your church, family, or friends—get in contact and rekindle that relationship. If the relationship requires forgiveness, today is the day to commit yourself to forgiveness. If you need healing, confront your past, get some healing, and let go. There is strength in staying in touch with your heritage.

PRAYER

Father in the name of Jesus, I make a fresh commitment to you to live in peace. I am letting go of bitterness, hurt, and unkindness. I ask for your forgiveness and release of all who have wronged me. Help me walk in love and peace. Help me behave myself towards others in a way that is gratifying to you. Amen.

DAY 3
Smooth Move

PREPARE FOR THE BATTLE...

*"Rejoice evermore. Pray without ceasing.
In every thing give thanks:
for this is the will of God in Christ
Jesus concerning you."*
1 THESSALONIANS 5:16-18

Were there times in your life when you made the wrong move or took matters into your own hands, and the outcome caused you a lot of hurt, disappointment, and anger? Girlfriend, get a pencil and paper. Write down the following equation: Event + response = outcome. Put it in your planners, tape it to your refrigerators, or email it to yourself. Our response to events affects their outcome. How are you handling things in your life—the missed promotion, the substance abuse, the depression, the emotional addiction. Whatever the challenges or battles may be, making the wrong move can be costly. Christ has given us the authority to be "smooth movers." Are you open to a new move? Are you open to new ways of approaching the challenges in your life? Here is a smooth move for you: pray, fast, believe, respond!

APPLICATION

By getting in touch with her past, Esther came to terms with God's purpose for her life. She stopped being fearful and uncertain and became confident and determined in her task. She prepared herself to face the challenge of saving her people. She pulled a smooth move! She pulled together some "sistahs" to pray, and she instructed Mordecai to have his people do the same.

Are you going through an unpredictable situation? Are you uncertain about what to do? Are there loved ones in your life who are at a crossroads? Today we are not going to rush into responding to the challenge. Today we are going to give it to God. Write down a challenging situation in your life you would like to see changed. Then let's follow Esther's example: Pull together some praying "sistahs." Let them in, "The Smooth Move." Pray about it. Fast. Believe God for his deliverance. Then respond!

www.urbanspirit.biz

PRAYER

Father, today we fast. Cleanse us from our sins. Prepare us to handle the circumstances in our lives. Remove fear and uncertainty and replace them with confidence and determination. Lord, today we give attention to your direction and your presence. We thank you for this day of preparation. In Jesus name, Amen.

DAY 4
Playing it cool
PATIENCE...

*"For this cause I bow my knees unto the Father
of our Lord Jesus Christ,
Of whom the whole family in heaven and earth
is named, That he would grant you,
according to the riches of his glory,
to be strengthened with might by his Spirit."*

EPHESIAN 3:14,15

When you know that your prayer is going to be answered, you can keep your cool. Have a meeting with your boss; keep your cool! Your husband has been laid off from his job. Don't panic; keep your cool! Someone is getting on your nerves. Don't cuss! Keep your cool! Remember, Event + Response = Outcome.

Yesterday we worked on becoming smooth movers. Let's praise God right now for the victories that are taking place in our lives. We've made the right moves, smooth moves, fasting, and believing-in-God-for-deliverance moves. Now what? Now we wait. We keep our cool, we believe, we expect a miracle, and we act as if we have received.

APPLICATION

Esther the queen prepared herself with prayer, fasting, and belief in God's deliverance. She put on her royal robes and approached the king with confidence and assurance. When the king saw Esther, his heart melted. He essentially told her that he would give her whatever she asked. Esther could have thrown herself into his arms kicking and screaming, "Save me! Save me!" But this Sistah was cool. This was her moment. She invited the king to a feast. While Esther and her maidservants were fasting and praying for deliverance, they were preparing a banquet! Talk about self-control.

When we ask God for deliverance, he wants us to have faith. He wants us to approach the situation as if our request has been answered. He wants us not to be anxious, depressed, or emotionally out of control. God wants us to play it cool.

Today we are going to play it cool. We are going to sit down calmly, by ourselves, and be alone with the Lord for a time of quietness. Turn off the TV. The soap operas and game shows will still be there later. Take time to come before God in peace and quiet. When you are at a crossroads, it helps to focus on the Lord. In the midst of your battles, listen to his quiet, tranquil, loving voice directing your path.

www.urbanspirit.biz

PATIENCE...

PRAYER

Lord, we thank you for this quiet time. Thank you for the intimacy we are having with you. Thank you for your spirit of calmness. We know that you will direct our paths; we know that you are working on the challenges in our lives. Thank you for calming our nerves and clearing our minds. In the name of Jesus. Amen.

DAY 5

Ya Got Played

Deliverance...

*"Cast thy burden upon the Lord,
and he shall sustain thee:
he shall never suffer the righteous
to be moved."*

PSALM 55:22

Will you be played or will you receive deliverance? I worked for years for a manager who did not believe in Jesus. She made my life really difficult. I prayed. I cried, "Lord deliver me!" I stayed right there. The more integrity I showed, the worse the situation got. This manager was determined to break my spirit. And the devil was busy in both of us. I did everything I knew to deal with this challenge. I meditated and focused on the inner woman. "Lord, please hold my tongue. Please don't let me cuss this manager out!" I had to pray for strength to maintain my Christian character. I stayed in touch with the Word of God. I did the smooth move, prayed, fasted, and continued to believe in the purpose and the power of God. I kept my cool. When I had done everything in my power to deal with the situation, God stepped in. His timing could not have been better. I am so glad we serve a right-on-time God.

When things got unbearable, God's mercy and strength outshined my dim situation. The last thing this manager said to me was, "You have a great deal of inner strength. Where does it come from?" I told her, "You have seen Jesus in me." She apologized and asked for prayer.

APPLICATION

Esther the queen kept her cool and invited the king and Haman to a banquet. The king again offered Esther anything that she wanted, even up to half of his kingdom (Esther 7:1-2). As Esther finally broke her silence, "If I have found favour in thy sight, O king, and if it please the king, let my life be given me at my petition, and my people at my request" (Esther 7:3). The tables were turned. Haman got played. He lost his life; hung from the same gallows he had built to hang Mordecai.

When we are going through adversities in our lives, patience is essential. We must trust God and know that he has a plan. Although it may seem that we are victims, we have the assurance from Christ that we are not victims. That is why we pray for our enemies.

Today take some time to think about the following: Focus on the inner woman of strength; know your history and make peace with your past. Prepare yourself before approaching the unique challenges in your life. Keep your cool; trust in God. Pray, fast, believe, and respond. Ask God for unshakable courage.

PRAYER

Heavenly Father, thank you for the modern-day Esther. Thank you for the women who can take time out for inner beauty and develop the spiritual woman. We thank you for the intimacy we have with you and for your relationship with us. Amen.

✓ GOALS

Become an US Urban Spirit! Publishing and Media Company Independent or Church Distributor Today!

- earn extra money
- engage with more people
- change lives
- join a winning team
- distribute high-quality Bibles and books

Go to www.urbanspirit.biz

Order your Independent or Church Distributor "Starter Kit" today online. It contains everything you need to get started selling right away.
Or call **800.560.1690** to get started today!

NOTES

NOTES

NOTES

NOTES

NOTES

NOTES

NOTES

NOTES

KING JAMES VERSION

WOMEN of COLOR
STUDY BIBLE